Foreword

When Shirley called me and asked me to write the Foreword for her book, I didn't know what to think, or even know what the foreword of a book was. Subsequently I've read many, however, not unless you are an editor you wouldn't think about the correct structure of a book. So like anyone else, I googled "Foreword", then I thought to myself, hummm?

SHIRLEY LARRIER, author – *"When Will the Morning Come?"* The Prison System in America. An astonishing book written about the businesses of the PRISON system (a serious multi-billion dollar industry), the complexity and bewildering process of how it's run, beyond belief, and who the players are!

Well, it comes as no surprise to me that Shirley, this tall statuesque, intelligent African American woman. Who walks into a room, automatically draws attention without saying a word, and later would become a magnet for those who can converse with her on life, would research such a compelling and riveting manuscript.

This book is totally opposite from the previous fiction book she has written. On numerous occasions, while doing the research, Shirley conveyed information and educated me, as well; enticing me to want to learn more; hunger for more. And that's precisely what she wants to do for her readers; to educate and enlighten them, and to learn the truth about what's happening behind the prison walls with our incarcerated people. With such heartfelt passion, Shirley's hunger to dig deeper and deeper into this topic, the magnitude of information she discovered about prison politics and the behavior, I could only imagined this book making the best sellers list.

I've known Shirley for my entire life. In the 1950's our families grew up together in Farragut Projects in Brooklyn. As a matter of fact, Shirley and my older sister Janet were the same age; they were friends and began their formal education together; both very, very intelligent and always eager to learn. Janet McDonald too, became an author and wrote her biography, Project Girl, and a series of other fiction books written for the adolescent reader before she passed away in 2007.

In much later years, during my early professional career, I ran into Shirley in the cafeteria of an employer whom we both worked for. She now became my friend and mentor. You see, Shirley had been working in Corporate America much longer than I. So she knew the ins and outs'; how to work to stay IN and if you didn't comply, you would be OUT! She was always very comical but intelligent and would always say **"See, I know how it go!"** I admired her drive, determination and confidence.

As my friend and mentor, while going through life's journey, she had another saying that she still says today, **"They don't do us right!"** and for the most part, she means our people. A quote that will inevitably be brought to light once you have read, *"When Will the Morning Come?"* The injustices of the prison system that you will read about in this book, will be shocking to some and more revealing to others.

Deborah McDonald-Jackson

Dedication

To all my African Black Brothers and Sisters who has been wrongly accused of crimes which they didn't commit. The only crime that you committed against society was being born an African Black, Brother or Sister. I fast and pray that this nightmare will be over for you very soon.

Hang in there, you are the most strong and powerful men/women of this planet.

"Never give up on raising the consciousness of our people"

Introduction

Before researching this book, I was sitting at my desk working, with one of the largest financial companies on Wall Street. Which, I don't care to mention their name. One of the Financial Analyst brought me a presentation they needed for a Merger & Acquisition (M&A) to secure a deal. This deal was based on a prison in NYS and the profit they would make. Here I was naive and ignorant. I said to myself who in their right mind would be interested in a prison. After reading the presentation, I realized this was not stupid at all. I was also told that anything that came across my desk was confidential, after receiving that presentation. I caught an instant attitude. I didn't know exactly what I was reading at first. About two years later listening to a talk show on the radio about our prison system it hit me again. I automatically became interested in the topic.

The United States now has approximately 2.3 million prisoners, and about 1 million are African Black men. In spite, of the fact that African black people represent about 13% of the population. If this present trends continue, 1 in 3 black men born today can look forward to going to prison in their lifetime.

As of January 2014 the New York State Department of Corrections and **Community Supervision**, guided by the **Departmental Mission**, is responsible for the confinement and rehabilitation of approximately 54,000 individuals under custody held at 54 state **facilities** and 36,000 parolees supervised through-out seven regional offices.[1]

Just a little bit of information for those who are not aware of our prison system, and how it functions. U.S. prisons are one of the biggest businesses we now have in the Americas. 47% of state prisoners are African American men, and 37.6% in federal prisons.[1,2]

We have been socially engineered into this dilemma, and the only way out is to be socially engineered, the same way we got in. We need to get out.

Types of incarceration

Federal prisons: Run by U.S. Bureau of Prisons; hold prisoners convicted of federal crimes and pretrial detainees.

State prisons: Run by state corrections departments; hold sentenced inmates serving time for felonies, usually longer than one year.

Local jails: County or municipal facilities; hold defendants prior to trial and those serving short sentences, usually less than one year.

Other types: Juvenile detention facilities, police lock-ups (small rooms in police stations where prisoners are held), immigration detention facilities, military prisons, state mental hospitals (when civilly committed).

"SLAVERY by Another Name"

Chain Gangs

In the early 1900s, dramatic stories of the abuse and wretched conditions of convict laborers began to be publicized through trials and newspaper accounts. The egregiousness of the violence and CORRUPTION of the system began to turn public opinion against convict leasing. Though many citizens and politicians wanted to abolish convict leasing, the problem of the expense and difficulty of housing convicts remained. Chain gangs developed as a popular solution to that problem.

Chain gangs were groups of convicts forced to labor at tasks such as road CONSTRUCTION, ditch digging, or farming while chained together. Some chain gangs toiled at work sites near the prison, while others were housed in transportable jails such as railroad cars or trucks. The improvements they made to public roadways had significant impact on rural areas, allowing planters to move quickly and more easily transport their crops to market.

Chain gangs minimized the cost of guarding prisoners, but exposed prisoners to painful ULCERS and dangerous infections from the heavy shackles around their ankles. An individual's misstep or fall could imperil the entire group, and chains prevented individuals from moving away from aggressive or violent prisoners. Chain gangs eventually gave way to work gangs – groups of prisoners who worked off-site and under guard, but not in chains.[3]

"The Prison State of America"

Chris Hedges. December 28, 2014

Prisons employ and exploit the ideal worker. Prisoners do not receive benefits or pensions. They are not paid overtime. They are forbidden to organize and strike. They must show up on time. They are not paid for sick days or granted vacations.

They cannot formally complain about working conditions or safety hazards. If they are disobedient, or attempt to protect their pitiful ways, they lose their jobs and can be sent to isolation cells. The roughly 1 million prisoners who work for corporations and government industries in the American prison system are models for what the corporate state expects us all to become. And corporations have no intention of permitting prison reforms that would reduce the size of their bonded workforce. In fact, they are seeking to replicate these conditions throughout the society.

States, in the name of austerity, have stopped providing prisoners with essential items including shoes, extra blankets and even toilet paper, while starting to charge them for electricity and room and board. Most prisoners and the families that struggle to support them are chronically short of money. Prisons are company towns. Scrip, rather than money, was once paid to coal miners, and it could be used only at the company store. Prisoners are in a similar condition. When they go broke–and being broken is a frequent occurrence in prison–prisoners must take out prison loans to pay for medications, legal and medical fees and basic commissary items such as soap and deodorant. Debt peonage inside prison is as prevalent as it is outside prison.

States impose an array of fees on prisoners. For example, there is a 10 percent charge imposed by New Jersey on every commissary purchase. Stamps have a 10 percent surcharge. Prisoners must pay the state for a 15-minute deathbed visit to an immediate family member or a 15-minute visit to a funeral home to view the deceased. New Jersey, like most other states, forces a prisoner to reimburse the system for overtime wages paid to the two guards who accompany him or her, plus mileage cost. The charge can be as high as $945.04. It can take years to pay off a visit with a dying father or mother.

Fines, often in the thousands of dollars, are assessed against many prisoners when they are sentenced. There are 22 fines that can be imposed in New Jersey, including the Violent Crime Compensation Assessment (VCCB), the Law Enforcement Officers Training & Equipment Fund (LEOT) and Extradition Costs (EXTRA). The state takes a percentage each month out of prison pay to pay down the fines, a process that can take decades. If a prisoner who is fined $10,000 at sentencing must rely solely on a prison salary he or she will earn about $4,000 after making payments for 25 years. Prisoners can leave prison in debt to the state. And if they cannot continue to make regular payments–difficult because of high unemployment–they are sent back to prison. High recidivism is part of the design.

Advertisement

Corporations have privatized most of the prison functions once handled by governments. They run prison commissaries and, since the prisoners have nowhere else to shop, often jack up prices by as much as 100 percent. Corporations have taken over the phone systems and charged exorbitant fees to prisoners and their families.

They grossly overcharge for money transfers from families to prisoners. And these corporations, some of the nation's largest, pay little more than a dollar a day to prison laborers who work in for-profit prison industries.

Food and merchandise vendors, construction companies, laundry services, uniforms companies, prison equipment vendors, cafeteria services, manufacturers of pepper spray, body armor and the array of medieval instruments used for the physical control of prisoners, and a host of other contractors feed like jackals off prisons. Prisons, in America, are hugely profitable business.

Our prison-industrial complex, which holds 2.3 million prisoners, or 25 percent of the world's prison population, MAKES MONEY by keeping prisons full. It demands bodies, regardless of color, gender or ethnicity. As the system drains the pool of black bodies, it has begun to incarcerate others.

Women—the fastest-growing segment of the prison population—are swelling prisons, as are poor whites in general, Hispanics and immigrants. Prisons are no longer a black-white issue. Prisons are a grotesque manifestation of corporate capitalism. Slavery is legal in prisons under the 13th Amendment of the U.S. Constitution. It reads: "Neither slavery nor involuntary servitude, except as punishment for crime whereof the party shall have been duly convicted, shall exist within the United States. ..." And the massive U.S. prison industry functions like the forced labor camps that have existed in all totalitarian states.

Corporate investors, who have poured billions into the business of mass incarceration, expect long-term returns. And they will get them. It is their lobbyists who write the draconian laws that demand absurdly long sentences, DENY paroles, determine immigrant detention laws and impose minimum-sentence and three-strikes-out laws (mandating life sentences after three felony convictions). The politicians and the courts, subservient to corporate power, can be counted on to protect corporate interests.

CORRECTIONS Corporation of America (CCA), the largest owner of for-profit prisons and immigration detention facilities in the country, had revenues of $1.7 billion in 2013 and profits of $300 million. CCA holds an average of 81,384 INMATES in its facilities on any one day. Aramark Holdings Corp., a Philadelphia-based company that contracts through Aramark Correctional Services to provide food to 600 correctional institutions across the United States, was acquired in 2007 for $8.3 billion by investors that included Goldman Sachs.[4]

6

Chapter 1

Reimagine! Movements Making Media

"Rooted in Slavery: Prison Labor Exploitation"
Jaron Browne

The United States has once again surpassed its own world record for incarcerating the highest percentage of its population. According to a report released by the Bureau of Prison Statistics, one out of every 32 adults was in prison, in jail, on probation, or on parole at the end of 2005. But the crisis of mass incarceration is not felt evenly in the United States: Race defines every aspect of the criminal justice system, from police targeting, to crimes charged, and rates of conviction. African-American men between the ages of 20 and 39 account for nearly one third of all sentenced prisoners.[1]

Over the last three decades, the explosion of the prison population in the United States paralleled the stagnation in the global economy. In the early 1970s, the United States and the G7 nations began implementing neoliberal policies, moving production from the North to the global South, pushing entire sectors of workers in the United States out of the economy. As the economic role of the working class in the United States shifted from manufacturing to staffing a rising service industry, African American workers faced staggering rates of unemployment. The mid-1970s is also the first period when the incarceration rate in the United States began to rise, doubling in the 1980s, and doubling again in the 1990s.

United States Prisons Mirror Free Enterprise Zones in Africa, Asia, and Latin America; the prison is a reflection of the Third World within the United States.

Prisoners are not protected by minimum wage laws or overtime, and are explicitly barred from the right to organize and collectively bargain. In fact, the conditions for the overwhelmingly Black and Latino men and women inside the United States prison system are so similar to that of workers in the maquiladoras and sweatshops of the global South that in 1995, Oregon politicians were even courting Nike to move their production from Indonesia into Oregon prisons. "We propose that (Nike) take a look at their transportation costs and their labor costs," Oregon State Representative Kevin Mannix explained in an interview with researcher Reese Erlich, "We could offer [competitive] prison inmate labor" in Oregon.[2]

Rooted in Slavery

To understand the conditions that have allowed such an exploitative industry to develop, we have to look at the origin of the United States prison system itself. Before the abolition of slavery there was no real prison system in the United States. Punishment for crime consisted of physical torture, referred to as corporal or capital punishment. While the model prison in the United States was built in Auburn, New York in 1817, it wasn't until the end of the Civil War, with the official abolition of slavery, that the prison system took hold.

In 1865, the 13th Amendment officially abolished slavery for all people except those convicted of a crime and OPENED the door for mass criminalization. Prisons were built in the South as part of the backlash to Black Reconstruction and as a mechanism to re-enslave Black workers. In the late 19th-century South, had an extensive prison system was developed in the interest of maintaining the racial and economic relationship of slavery.

Louisiana's famous Angola Prison illustrates this HISTORY best. In 1880, this 8000-acre family plantation was purchased by the state of Louisiana and converted into a prison.

Slave quarters became cell units. Now expanded to 18,000 acres, the Angola plantation is tilled by prisoners working the land—a chilling picture of modern day chattel slavery.

Black Codes and Convict Leasing

When slavery was legally abolished, a new set of laws called the Black Codes emerged to criminalize legal activity for African Americans. Through the enforcement of these laws, acts such as standing in one area of town or walking at night, for example, became the criminal acts of "loitering" or "breaking curfew," for which African Americans were imprisoned. As a result of Black Codes, the percentage of African Americans in prison grew exponentially, surpassing whites for the first time.[3]

A system of convict leasing was developed to allow white slave plantation owners in the South to literally purchase prisoners to live on their property and work under their control. Through this system, bidders paid an average $25,000 a year to the state, in exchange for control over the lives of all of the prisoners. The system provided revenue for the state and profits for plantation owners. In 1878, Georgia leased out 1,239 prisoners, and all but 115 were African American.[4]

Much like the system of slavery from which it emerged, convict leasing was a violent and abusive system. The death rate of prisoners leased to railroad companies between 1877 and 1879 was 16 percent in Mississippi, 25 percent in Arkansas, and 45 percent in South Carolina.[5]

The stories of violence and torture eventually led to massive reform and abolition movements involving alliances between prisoner organizations, labor unions, and community groups. By the 1930s, every state had abolished convict leasing.[6]

Chain Gangs

As the southern states began to phase out convict leasing, prisoners were increasingly made to work in the most brutal form of forced labor, the chain gang. The chain gangs originated as a part of a massive road development project in the 1890s. Georgia was the first state to begin using chain gangs to work male felony convicts outside of the prison walls. Chains were wrapped around the ankles of prisoners, shackling five together while they worked, ate, and slept. Following Georgia's example, the use of chain gangs spread rapidly throughout the South.[7]

For over 30 years, African American prisoners (and some white prisoners) in the chain gangs were worked at gunpoint under whips and chains in a public spectacle of chattel slavery and torture. Eventually, the brutality and violence associated with chain gang labor in the United States gained worldwide attention. The chain gang was abolished in every state by the 1950s, almost 100 years after the end of the Civil War.[8]

Prison Labor Exploitation in the 21st Century

Just a few decades later, we are witnessing the return of all of these systems of prison labor exploitation. Private corporations are able to lease factories in prisons, as well as lease prisoners out to their factories. Private corporations are running prisons-for-profit. Government-run prison factories operate as multibillion dollar industries in every state, and throughout the federal prison system.

In the most punitive and racist prison systems, we are even witnessing the return of the chain gang. Prisoner resistance and community organizing has been able to defeat some of these initiatives, but in Arizona, Maricopa County continues to operate the first women's chain gang in the history of the United States.[9]

Shifts in the United States economy and growing crises of underemployment and poverty in communities of color have created the conditions for the current wave of mass incarceration and the boom in prison labor exploitation. In the Bay view Hunters Point neighborhood of San Francisco, a historically Black community with an estimated 50 percent unemployment rate, the community is facing criminalization, incarceration and mass displacement as a result of gentrification. San Francisco, along with eight other counties in California, is implementing gang injunctions—curfews, anti-loitering, and anti-association laws that function very similar to Black Codes for Black, Latino, and Asian youth—using the pretext of gang prevention to track young men into the prison system to become prison labor, while preparing the community for redevelopment and gentrification. People Organized to Win Employment Rights (POWER) is building power among Bay view residents and fighting for economic development that addresses the interests of the Black community, which will create alternatives to prison labor exploitation.[10]

Struggles like this are being waged all across the country and provide an opening to link the demands for worker rights, community rights, and prisoner rights.

The fight against the exploitation of prison labor is at once a fight against racial profiling and mass incarceration, and also for genuine economic development in Black, Latino, Asian, and Pacific Islander communities.

The labor movement in the United States has a responsibility to support prisoner unions such as the Missouri Prison Labor Union (MPLU), which is fighting for higher wages and collective bargaining, and to challenge labor unions that dismiss prisoners as stealing jobs from the "good law-abiding workers" on the outside. As Sidney Williams of the MLPU states, "In this struggle we seek to regain our human dignity." That is the demand of the slavery abolition movement of the 21st century.

Chapter 2

"Black Men Are Missing: Tell Us Something We Don't Know"
The Root – Peniel E. Joseph, April 27 2015

The New York Times has documented the "disappearance" of black men for the past decades through mass incarceration and death, but brings no solutions to the discussion.

The tragic and spiraling plight of black men in American society has reached such epic proportions that the national paper of record, the New York Times, is discussing the "disappearance" of African-American men from civil society. "The stigmatization of blackness presents an enormous obstacle," it notes, "even to small boys."

The editorial, "Forcing Black Men out of Society," followed on the heels of another Times story that found 1.5 million African-American men were "missing" from everyday life because of incarceration and early death, leaving devastated communities, impoverished families, and a cycle of stigma, shame and hopelessness in their wake. The numbers are startling: For every 100 black women ages 25-54 who are not incarcerated, there are only 83 men. In Ferguson, Mo., that number shrinks to 60.

The New York Times analysis and editorial noting that 1 in 6 black men have simply disappeared from daily life in America are noteworthy because this trend, although not new, is receiving a second look by politicians, policymakers and the general public in light of the spate of police shootings of blacks and the subsequent #BlackLivesMatter movement that galvanized the nation last year.

The new racial caste system thrives more on mass incarceration than even early death because inordinate amounts of time spent in prison during the past three decades have robbed the African-American community of the potential civic, economic and familial contributions of at least two generations of black men.

For those unfamiliar with the story, the basic narrative goes something like this: In the aftermath of 1960s-era civil rights victories, African-American men fell victim to global economic shifts that turned major cities into postindustrial wastelands. Jobs, tax bases and opportunities shifted to the suburbs, out West and overseas, leaving behind a desperate, largely UNEMPLOYABLE, surplus labor force.

The war on drugs added grave and enduring insult to this pre-existing injury, trapping hundreds of thousands of black men in the bowels of the new American gulag. During the 1980s and 1990s, the black poor was labeled a new racial "underclass," even as prominent scholars, most notably sociologist William Julius Wilson, insisted that the disappearance of work, more than black behavior, was at the root of the economic misery that contoured African-American inner cities.

So this story is not new, since, as the Times put it, "every census for the last 50 years has shown the phenomenon" of missing black men.

What is new, however, and perhaps offers a sign of hope, is a re-energized discussion over race, class, poverty and criminal justice. The Times editorial offered no policy suggestions other than QUOTING Wilson's two-decades-long advocacy for a New Deal-style Works Progress Administration program that would offer every man government-sponsored public employment.

A WPA-styled policy intervention, combined with new legislation aimed at dismantling the system of mass incarceration, would be the kind of bold, ambitious and concrete policy agenda that could untie the Gordian knot of racial injustice in which these missing black men find themselves caught up.

The Times should be applauded for these and other stories that have offered a depth of analysis and reporting on the way in which America's sprawling system of racial and economic justice does grievous injury and harm to black communities. Pain that, sociologist Michael Eric Dyson reminds us, can be lightning quick or maddeningly SLOW.

The #BlackLivesMatter movement deserves special praise for its unrelenting and heroic commitment to both protesting the vast spectrum of anti-black racism across the nation and offering concrete policy demands for how we can begin the long road toward genuine racial justice and economic opportunity in America.

There is something profoundly sad about the fact that it takes the combination of prolific and videotaped police shootings of black men and bone-rattling national protests to inspire such coverage in the Times.

Welcome to black America's reality, a place where African-American men, women and children live daily with the loss of brothers, fathers, husbands, caretakers, friends and mentors. The human cost cannot be adequately measured in numbers alone.

Now, more than ever, we need policy solutions for jobs, decriminalizing black men and women, and injecting resources and hope in neighborhoods and communities, most recently Baltimore and Ferguson that are exploding in protests and unrest after being burdened for decades by racial segregation, UNEMPLOYMENT, police brutality and stigma.

Places with the lowest rates	Place PCT. Black Men
Ferguson, Mo.	37.5%
Shaker Heights, Ohio	38.1%
Highland Springs, Va.	38.3%
Westmont, Calif.	38.3%
Farmington Hills, Mich.	39.0%
Union City, Ga.	39.1%
Euclid, Ohio	39.3%
Oak Park, Mich.	39.3%
East Chicago, Ind.	39.4%
Garfield Heights, Ohio	39.6%

In places with at least 10,000 black residents

Places with most missing men	Place PCT. Black Men	"Missing"
New York	43.1%	118,000
Chicago	43.4%	45,000
Philadelphia	42.8%	36,000
Detroit	45.2%	21,000
Memphis	43.6%	21,000
Baltimore	44.0%	19,000
Houston	45.5%	18,000
Charlotte, N.C.	43.3%	15,000
Milwaukee	42.2%	14,000
Dallas	44.8%	13,000

http://users.nber.org/~jwolfers/popular/Upshot/1.5%20Million%20Missing%20Black%20Men%20-%20NYTimes.pdf

Chapter 3

"Prisoners for Profit: CUNY Prison Divest and the Carceral State"

Christina Nadler, Melissa Martuano, and Sean M. Kenned, April 29, 2015

Through a Freedom of Information Law (FOIL) request, CUNY Prison Divest, a new cross-campus coalition of student-organizers working towards divestment from PRIVATE prisons, was able to CONFIRM that CUNY's endowment has substantial investments in private-prison companies. These investments include the Geo Group, Inc. (with endowment holdings of $8,400 USD), Corrections Corporation of America (CCA; $13,300 USD), and G4S ($248,900 USD). CUNY is also invested in at least one major prison contractor, Aramark ($4,600 USD), and Wall Street firms that have at least one million private-prison shares apiece, including Wells Fargo ($743,800 USD) and Morgan Stanley ($157,500 USD). Though CUNY's revenue comes primarily through state and city funding as well as tuition, CUNY's endowment plays an increasingly important role as university fundraising from private donors increases as public funding decreases.

Ashley Agbasoga, a Brooklyn College senior and one of the main organizers of CUNY Prison Divest, and Ian Trupin, a full-time organizer with the Responsible Endowments Coalition and a fellow core organizer of CUNY Prison Divest, gave an interview to Christina Nadler (sociology), Melissa Marturano (classics), and Sean M. Kennedy (English), all Graduate Center doctoral students, regarding this pressing issue.

We (Christina, Melissa, and Sean) hope this interview can raise awareness in the GC community about CUNY's investments in private prisons, mobilize our community to protest these investments with CUNY Prison Divest, and enable us to think more critically about the need for the abolition of all prisons.

As Ashley discusses in her responses to our questions, prisons and the prison system (known as the prison-industrial complex because of its extensive links to state and private capital) tear APART, terrorize, and incapacitate communities that are composed predominantly of poor people of color. Prisons do not make us safe. They are horrific manifestations of both state and capitalist violence.

Christina Nadler [CN]: What's wrong with PRIVATE prisons? Why do you want CUNY to divest from them? And how does this link up to other divestment efforts, such as from fossil fuels or from the Israeli occupation of Palestine?

Ian Trupin [IT]: The leading private-prison companies are GEO Group and CCA, which collectively hold contracts for about three-fourths of the private-prison beds in this country. Their combined revenues were over $3 billion USD in 2012. There are other private-prison companies, like MTC and G4S, but these haven't been targeted as frequently because MTC stock is not traded publicly on the stock market and G4S is a gigantic global corporation (the second largest after WALMART) and private prisons and detention centers are a relatively small part of their business.

Ashley Agbasoga [AA]: Prison as a concept is horribly wrong. But when you're literally profiting off of the lives of others, it's disgusting. People in both state and private prisons are usually put in there for injustices and unfair policies – for instance, most people incarcerated are in for non-violent crimes and they [are facing] extremely long sentences. You can find out more about the many abuses people face in private prisons, such as the denial of medical care and physical assault, in an online article from ACLU called "Warehoused and Forgotten."

And the first reading that got me into this is Michelle Alexander's *The New Jim Crow*. That sparked my interest in the prison-industrial complex as a whole and the policies around it. Keep an OPEN mind for critiques, but there is a lot of writing out there on this subject. As for why we want CUNY to divest, I don't want money [from] public education going towards imprisoning my own communities. I identify as Black and I know how prisons affect our communities firsthand – [they've] affected my own family, and I have seen what it can do to my friends and neighbors here in Brooklyn. I wouldn't want my school to fund these institutions that destroy my community. In terms of working with other groups, I personally work with Students for Justice for Palestine, and the Boycott, Divestment, and Sanctions (BDS) movement. A lot of CUNY Prison Divest core members are also in other movements, such as Students for a Democratic Society, and Students for Justice for Palestine, and other Palestinian-rights organizations.

IT: G4S is also a BDS target, and climate change is becoming a leading factor contributing to the displacement of people, which GENERATES INCOME for prison companies who lock up climate refugees in detention centers. The Israeli occupation of Palestine functions as a laboratory for private companies like G4S to develop new systems of control, including carceral and surveillance technologies that are then marketed for profit around the world.

Sean M. Kennedy [SMK]: Can you give us a snapshot of the status of the movement against PRIVATE prisons in the United States generally and at CUNY specifically? And how is CUNY part of the national movement?

AA: The private-prison movement is relatively new. There have been several abolitionist groups that want the abolition of all prisons, private or public, [but] private prisons didn't get a lot of attention until recently. CUNY Prison Divest started with the help of Ian. I met him at a Columbia Prison Divest EVENT, and we thought it'd be a great idea to bring this to CUNY. I went to Columbia my first year of undergrad, and a lot of the founders of Columbia Prison Divest I was personally friends with. I thought, Wouldn't it be a good idea to see if CUNY is investing? I bet they are. So we started a coalition group. We reached out to other groups that participate in social-justice movements. Now we're growing strong. We got our Freedom of Information Law (FOIL) request back; we're planning teach-ins on our campuses. We definitely have to approach it differently than at Columbia because Columbia's more of a nuclear campus as opposed to CUNY, which is massive with schools all over the five boroughs. So we're still in the planning stages of how to effectively make this work. We're going to make a solid plan before we go out there.

IT: CUNY Prison Divest is CONNECTED with the National Prison Divestment Campaign, which was convened in 2011 to specifically use divestment as a means to destroy private prisons' ability to lobby for laws and contracts that are contributing to driving up mass incarceration. The national campaign was convened by Enlace, an organization made up of low-wage worker centers in the United States and Mexico, and over the four years of its existence has included over 150 organizations, including grassroots groups, unions, [and] media campaigning and advocacy groups. CUNY Prison Divest members have taken part in regional and national prison divestment convening's and other events.

Melissa Marturano [MM]: Private-prison companies particularly receive a lot of attention because of their role in immigration-detention centers along the US-Mexico border. These companies are exploiting the US' ever-increasing militarized and draconian immigration laws and the federal government's shift from deportation to indefinite detention—they see immigrant detention as a "growth industry" and lobby aggressively to ensure that immigration laws become harsher and harsher.

AA: Absolutely. These private-prison companies have facilities that detain undocumented immigrants and immigrants waiting on their asylum applications. The conditions in these prisons are obviously inhumane, and should especially not be happening to families. Women and children being detained in the South-west face unbearable conditions. It's definitely a profitable market, and in a capitalist society, we have entities like private prisons that profit off people's lives. Instead of deportations – which are also wrong – they're MAKING MONEY by keeping people in the system, which is terrifying.

MM: I just read in Colorlines about a hunger and work strike by women at the PRIVATE Karnes Immigrant Detention Center run by the GEO Group. The women there have little access to clean water unless they buy a bottle of water, which costs three dollars a bottle – more than they make from a day of work. I'm curious as to how much attention this is going to get, especially since these are women striking. This is something Victoria Law writes about – too often people only pay attention to the resistance of men behind bars, but as we imprison and detain more and more women in this country, is that going to shift?

AA: I hope there's a shift soon! I'm already seeing dialogue around looking at the imprisonment of women in our country and how it affects communities en masse; however, there's clearly not enough out there that shifts the conversation to how women are directly and indirectly affected by mass incarceration.

CUNY Prison Divest has CONNECTIONS TO CUNY Dreamers and Families for Freedom, other immigrant rights groups and they keep us posted about things going on within immigrant communities in New York. In the future, we would like to start addressing Immigration and Customs Enforcement (ICE) detention centers in New York.

MM: One of the main criticisms against private prisons — the same for neoliberal, corporate entities like charter schools — is their lack of any real transparency or oversight, which allows for egregious abuses. But egregious abuses happen all the time in state- and federal-run facilities as well. The state can, too, hide in the shadows and can cover its abuse with legal sanction. Is CUNY Prison Divest going to research whether CUNY has any financial or institutional ties to state-run prisons, which are the majority of prisons in the United States? Or is the idea to TARGET private prisons first, then public ones, as part of the broad prison-abolition movement?

AA: As a group, CUNY Prison Divest is definitely interested in examining how our school system is involved in state-run prisons. Prisons at all levels, whether they are public or private, contribute to the mass incarceration that TARGETS large numbers in Black and Brown communities. Tackling all prisons could definitely prove to be an arduous task. I, however, believe that it is imperative to tackle all prisons, as they all contribute to the devastating mass incarceration in our country.

To be quite honest, private or public prisons all eventually have the same goal – to incarcerate. Private prisons obviously do it for a profit, but there is plenty of money in publicly operated prisons as well. Currently, we as CUNY Prison Divest are only tackling private prisons since we have a direct investment that has been proven through the FOIL request, but hope to eventually have our school system divest from all forms of prisons.

MM: Ruth Wilson Gilmore, a CUNY professor, recently wrote in the Social Justice Journal about four issues she saw in the movement against mass incarceration and for prison abolition; one of them being what she believes is an undue emphasis on PRIVATE prisons and divestment from them at UNIVERSITIES. If only "about 5 percent of the people locked up are doing time in private prisons," according to Gilmore, then public prisons and jails, which hold the other 95% of incarcerated people, should receive more attention. What is CUNY Prison Divest's response to this critique? This is something I personally grapple with all the time as an activist – is our energy in the wrong place? Is there a wrong place to focus in the face of obvious injustice?

AA: This is something I grapple with too. Sometimes, I do think that it may be a waste of time to go after private prisons when they make up such a small percentage of the prisons in America. However, private prisons are growing at an astronomical rate, much faster than public prisons. Their tactics and their partnerships with the state [are troubling]. Private prisons should not be profiting off communities and bodies. Because they are growing at such an alarming rate that explains to me why so many people focus on them. How much are they charging the state to run these prisons? And sometimes, the conditions are much, much worse in private prisons than they are in state-run prisons. Eventually, CUNY Prison Divest wants to make sure CUNY is not involved in any prisons.

IT: I think that Professor Gilmore's point of view doesn't reflect an accurate analysis of the goals and strategy of the private-prison divestment campaign, which is focused on using divestment from private prisons to attack the lobbying influence of private companies, which has an effect well beyond the number of people currently locked up in private prisons.

Ironically, given her critique, the prison divestment campaign's stated goal is entirely about the state and the political process that is feeding mass incarceration. If anything, I believe a weakness is that divestment only focuses on the politics, and in itself will not set anyone free. However, divestment is one strategy with a proven track record in the fight against South African apartheid, tobacco companies, and now fossil fuels and Israeli apartheid. In each of these fights, divestment was and CONTINUES to be extremely effective in polarizing and activating society around these issues through our institutions like universities, unions, religious centers, and city governments. Also, this critique ignores immigration detention. Detention centers and prisons are similar and play similar roles. The drug war and the war on immigrants are branches from the same tree. And fifty percent of detention centers are privately run. The figures Gilmore cites are arrived at by ignoring immigrants in detention.

MM: For me, just from an immigration-rights standpoint, PRIVATE prisons need be stamped out immediately. As the United States detains more and more people at the US-Mexico border, more and more of these facilities will be OPENED up, which should be troubling for anyone – although, of course, all detention and deportation should be stamped out.

CN: As we start to look at the scope of these companies and these further connections, we could also broaden that scope to think about the other companies that MAKE MONEY from private prisons. Will CUNY Prison Divest also target the 36 companies, like Wells Fargo, that invest in private prisons?

AA: We've been in discussion about this but we haven't made a final decision. There are a lot of opposing viewpoints on what to do. Initially, before we filed the FOIL request, we knew that the CUNY Board of Trustees and other people who are important players in the CUNY system had ties to BANKS that are tied to private prisons – we knew that right off the bat.

But we also agreed that it would be much harder to go after these large banks rather than these private prisons. When the FOIL request came back and we got the percentages of CUNY's investments, starting with the private-prison groups instead of the larger entities made the most sense. However, we will not fail to mention that they have a large role in this system as well.

MM: So, for CUNY Prison Divest, it's a question of energy at this point — what can you do immediately and what you can do over the longer term?

SMK: Yeah, it sounds like a strategy of escalation, which is always a good strategy.

CN: As I understand it, the national movement's strategy focuses on endowments, but does the endowment strategy make as much sense for a public university like CUNY, which has a much smaller endowment ($300 million USD) than private universities typically do? Is there discussion in this movement about varied forms of investment in private prisons, beyond endowments?

AA: That's a really good question. Columbia's endowment is $9.23 billion USD. It's a ridiculous amount of MONEY.

CN: Especially when you compare it to CUNY's endowment.

AA: But the frank answer to this question is I don't care if CUNY's endowment was five dollars. If one dollar is going towards the imprisonment of people, especially if it's people who look like me, I don't want it in their endowment. No matter how "small" the endowment is there are much better things to invest in than private prisons. We take our model from Columbia because they are the closest to us and [have] the largest [campaign] in the Northeast; however, we always talk and debate about the way CUNY is very different. Our set-up is very different, from our endowment to the way things work at the board of trustees, to even just us being a public university.

Also, the demographics of CUNY are different than Columbia's and so, private-prison and SECURITY SYSTEMS will affect us much more as CUNY students. Even graduating with a CUNY degree as a person of color is different than [graduating with] a Columbia degree. And of course there are a lot things at play, if you have a Columbia ID you are going to be treated differently. Personally, I've gotten out of getting a ticket because I showed my old Columbia ID. CUNY is made up of working class people of color – though that's changing rapidly – and a lot of the students come from communities that are affected directly by police violence. We definitely have to look at those differences.

IT: I think this is a great question. Two campaigns that emerged this spring, at Middlebury College and Brown University, are demanding both prison divestment and abolition of the box on admissions forms that ask applicants if they've ever been convicted of a crime. I think these demands go well together as they can both become powerful ways to challenge our institution's complicity in mass incarceration. I have much less certainty about looking at prison labor, however. While I think it's really important to educate people about the EXISTENCE of slave labor in prisons, I've also heard that prison-labor programs in some instances are the only place people inside can get anything close to skills training, or even an activity to pass the time. This is not to say that prison-labor conditions aren't slavery, or that they aren't abusive or even sometimes dangerous for people inside. But I would encourage folks not to boycott prison products unless people on the inside specifically call upon us to do so in solidarity, which I haven't heard of yet.

SMK: In addition to endowment investments, a lot of universities have board members who are CONNECTED TOPRIVATE prisons. Do you know if any CUNY board members or administrators are linked to private prisons?

AA: We're currently in a research phase in determining [if any] board members are involved directly with private prisons. We have a little bit of research on which trustees are involved in certain banks, such as Wells Fargo.

CN: Recently, divestment from fossil fuels was discussed by the CUNY board of trustees subcommittee on investments and it received a lot of negative feedback from the board because, as members of the board claimed, it would be too great a loss of MONEY and, thus, they felt it would harm students. How do you hope to combat this mentality from the administration in your efforts to divest from private prisons?

AA: We know this is possibly going to be an argument against us. In terms of this, if I had to stand in front of the board of trustees, I would ask, "Can you think of anything else that will affect the CUNY population in terms of the cost of life more than PRIVATE prisons and fossil fuels? I'm pretty sure you can't." However, these investments are profitable and, so, I think we also have to think of where the CUNY system puts its MONEY. For example, inordinately high investments go into Macaulay Honors College, which really isn't meant to better the general CUNY student body but rather makes CUNY look like NYU or Columbia. We see that time and again within the CUNY system. So I would let them know that there are other things we can INVEST in.

IT: Ultimately, what matters is that people get free, and divestment just happens to be an effective political tool to mobilize university communities in this direction.

Also, divestment can take on added impact if the funds that are divested are reinvested in cooperatives or other businesses that hire formerly incarcerated people, or are redirected towards SCHOLARSHIPS and programs for communities that are targeted by ICE, the police, and the school-to-prison pipeline.

CN: And I think what you said before ties into this – prisons, private or state, are real issues for the majority of CUNY students who are largely working class students of color. So if you think of it that way, what will harm students more, possibly making less money in the endowment, or the private-prison and immigration-detention industry?

MM: The administration can justify not divesting by saying it harms students but, to me, that's just a line they say in ORDER to not think about it critically.

SMK: And endowment gains aren't going to students—it's just a mystifying discourse. More money could in fact benefit us, but it doesn't.

IT: If we invest in prisons, that means we're betting that prisons will continue to be profitable in the foreseeable future. For prisons to continue to be profitable, that means that racialized mass incarceration, the drug war, and the war on immigrants will have to continue. So a bet on private prisons is a bet against the communities and even the very lives of many in the CUNY community, which is majority people of color and working class. So, board of trustees, are you going to keep on betting that the captivity of our people will remain profitable?

CN: Looking at THE LIST of companies CUNY's invested in, I was wondering if CUNY divested from private prisons, would they move that money into industrialized slaughter houses, or into Smith & Wesson and the other problematic companies CUNY's invested in? Though now that we ask this question, perhaps we shouldn't even engage with this line of questioning because it's beside the point?

SMK: Yeah, because this is just a discursive tactic by the administration meant to mystify the issue. Answering this question isn't the point. The point is that we're proposing an ethical refusal. It's not up to us to know where to put the money, we just know we don't want the money invested in this.

This is the same question around Palestine. People always ask, "Why Palestine?" The answer – people are asking us to do this. Opponents always want to pivot to the question of why not boycott everything? Why not divest from everything? The point is, this is where the mobilization is, in these particular campaigns. Prison abolition is a linchpin for broad social transformation.

AA: We need to start somewhere. A huge force in Brown and Black communities is the power of the police and how institutionalized racism tears APART our communities [which prisons feed off of]. If we present facts about the private-prison industry, how deeply it's connected to politicians, and how the politicians we elect benefit from incarcerating communities of color, that's somewhere to start rather than just demanding the overthrow of capitalism, because people will ask, "Why?" For instance, many politicians, like Jerry Brown in California, receive campaign donations from private-prison corporations, and, thus, they create a partnership with these groups. Going against private prisons and the entire prison-industrial complex will open up questions about capitalism. This could spark something. For a lot of people, private prisons help them to ask those questions.

CN: For people who are reading this interview and becoming aware (or more aware) of this campaign, how can they get involved in CUNY Prison Divest?

AA: The first thing that pops into my head other than come to the meetings is read more, like the ACLU article I mentioned, "Warehoused and Forgotten," and ask questions. Go home and read about private prisons and come out to our meetings, they're usually at 7pm on Wednesdays. They're hosted in different parts of the city. There's a Facebook group, and we're working on building a WEBSITE. We also have a listserv. We'd love to see new faces and have people come in and join the fight.

Corrections Corp. of America stock jump

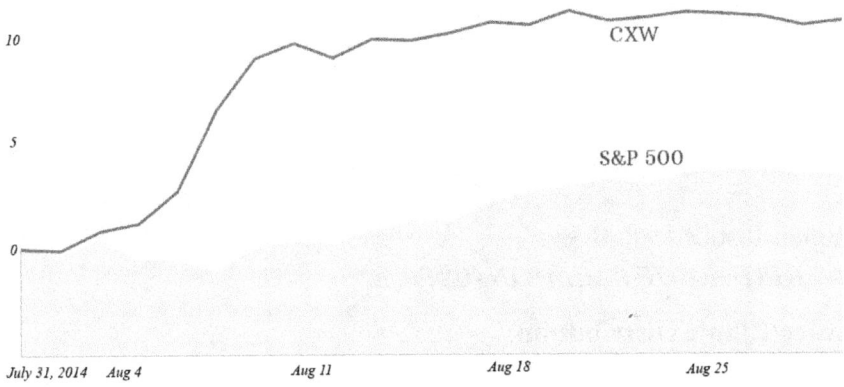

15 Percent

10

5

0

CXW

S&P 500

July 31, 2014   Aug 4   Aug 11   Aug 18   Aug 25

Chapter 4

Equal Justice Initiative
"A HISTORY OF RACIAL INJUSTICE"

Race/Ethnic Distribution

Almost half (49%) of the total offenders under custody on January 1, 2014 were African American with just under a quarter Hispanic and another quarter identified as White. A larger proportion of the female under custody population were White (41%) as compared to the male under custody population (23%). The incarcerated parolee population was more likely than the inmate population to be White (46% vs. 24%). Something is definitely wrong with this picture. For those of us who know and don't know, men most productive years are between 21-35 years old. Examine the graphic below:[1]

Age by Offender Status (2014)

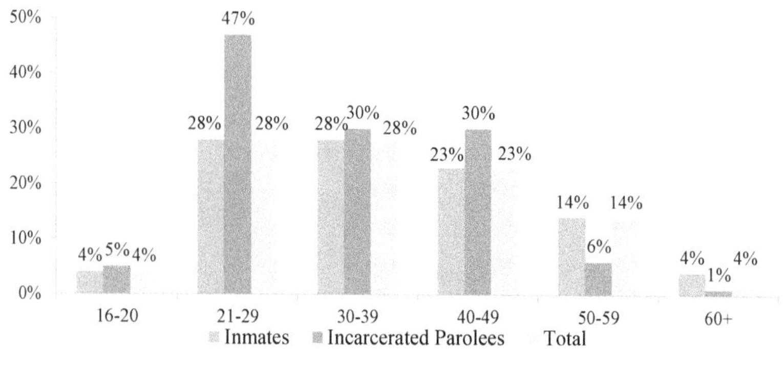

13th Amendment to the U.S. Constitution

The 13th Amendment to the Constitution declared that "Neither slavery nor involuntary servitude, except as a punishment for crime whereof the party shall have been duly convicted. It shall exist within the United States, or any place subject to their jurisdiction." Formally abolishing slavery in the United States, the 13th Amendment was passed by the Congress on January 31, 1865, and ratified by the states on December 6, 1865.

DECEMBER 18th, 1865

Ratification of the Thirteenth Amendment is announced

A constitutional amendment to forever abolish slavery was first proposed in the United States Congress in December 1863, during the Civil War and just months after President Abraham Lincoln's Emancipation Proclamation declared enslaved black people in rebelling states free. **Though the proclamation was a war measure that the government had little ability to enforce because it applied only in states that had declared themselves a separate nation**, an emancipation amendment would concretely establish slavery as contrary to the foundational principles of the United States. The Senate passed the abolition amendment on April 8, 1864. After an initial vote against it, months of debate and negotiations, and President Lincoln's re-election in 1864, the House passed the amendment on January 31, 1865.

Before the amendment could be added to the Constitution, two-thirds of the states – 27 out of the then-total 36 – had to ratify it. Northern states quickly did so. Many Southern states were reluctant but slowly joined suit after the April 1865 Confederate surrender and the passage of federal legislation that conditioned readmission to the Union on ratification of the amendment. On December 6, 1865, Georgia became the 27th state to approve ratification. On December 18, 1865, Secretary of State William H. Seward announced that the Thirteenth Amendment to the United States Constitution had been officially approved.

The amendment's text prohibits slavery and involuntary servitude except as punishment for crime, and that exception has proven a dangerous loophole. Many Southern states in the late 19th and early 20th centuries passed laws authorizing the "leasing" of (predominately black) state prisoners, who worked for no pay, in inhumane and deadly conditions, often while serving unjust sentences. As recently as 2010, in Serra v. Lappin, a federal court cited the Thirteenth Amendment in rejecting a lawsuit filed by federal prisoners, holding that "prisoners have no enforceable right to be paid for their work under the Constitution."

"Equal Justice Initiative, A History of Racial Injustice Timeline, at http://racialinjustice.eji.org/timeline/1860s/."

NOVEMBER 9th, 1866

Texas Legislature Authorizes Leasing of County Jail Inmates for Profit

The Thirteenth Amendment to the United States Constitution, ratified in December 1865, was then and is still frequently celebrated as the legislative act that ended American slavery. However, the amendment's text includes an exception:

"Neither slavery nor involuntary servitude, except as a punishment for crime whereof the party shall have been duly convicted, shall exist within the United States, or any place subject to their jurisdiction."

In Southern states that had long relied on the system of slavery to provide a constant labour supply for performing the agricultural work on which the region's economy was based and to buttress the social and political system of white supremacy, emancipation turned the system upside down. The constitutional provision permitting the continued enslavement of convicted criminals, however, provided a means of continued labour exploitation, and many states took it. In addition to passing "black codes" that criminalized acts like unemployment and public assembly when committed by freedmen, many Southern states also passed laws authorizing the leasing of the larger, predominately black convict populations these statutes created. Rather than create a financial burden for the state, increased prison populations could create profit.

In Texas, a law entitled "An Act to provide for the employment of Convicts for petty offenses" was approved on November 9, 1866, and authorized county authorities to employ jail inmates in public works and/or lease them out to private employers. Inmates were to receive a "wage" of one dollar per day, applied toward unpaid fines or costs owed to the county. Just days later, the legislature passed another law, authorizing the leasing of state prisoners. The arrangements would prove profitable for the state and deadly for the convicts, nearly all black, who were forced to work in dangerous, inhumane conditions.[2]

Region of Commitment

Approximately half (46%) of the offenders under custody on January 1, 2014 were committed from New York City and 11% were committed from suburban New York (Nassau, Rockland, Suffolk, and Westchester counties). Upstate counties with a population center of 50,000 inhabitants or more (Albany, Broome, Erie, Monroe, Oneida, Onondaga, Niagara, Rensselaer, and Schenectady counties) comprised 25% of the under custody population. The remaining 19% were sentenced from the other Upstate counties. The incarcerated parolee population was less likely than inmates to have been committed from New York City (19% vs. 46%) and more likely to have been committed from Upstate other counties (42% vs. 19%). When compared with males under custody, females under custody were less likely to come from New York City (34% vs. 46%) and were more likely to come from Upstate other (30% vs. 18%). [1]

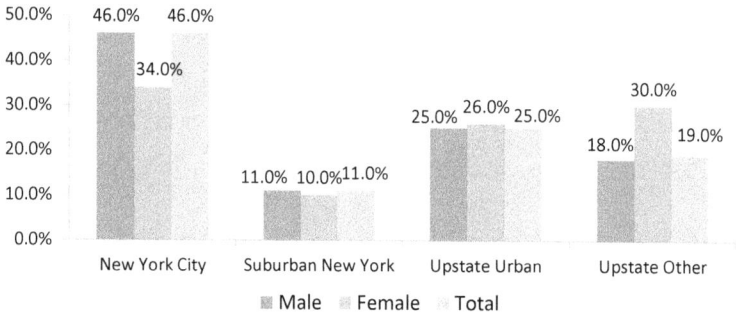

Maximum Sentence

As of January 1, 2014, the median maximum sentence of offenders under custody was 7 years (84 months). However, the average maximum sentence length was over eleven and a half years, reflecting the influence of lengthy maximum terms of many inmates. Almost a third had maximum sentences of 15 years or more with over 18% of the population having a maximum sentence of life. [1]

Average maximum sentences for women (99 months) were 42 months shorter than for men (141 months). Median maximum sentences for women (60 months) were 24 months shorter than for men (84 months). Average maximum sentences for inmates (141 months) were 93 months shorter than for incarcerated parolees (48 months).

In calculating the average maximum sentence length, "Life without Parole" cases were given a value of 45 years or 540 months, and Life maximum cases were given a value of 25 years or 300 months. [1]

Maximum Sentence Length of Offenders

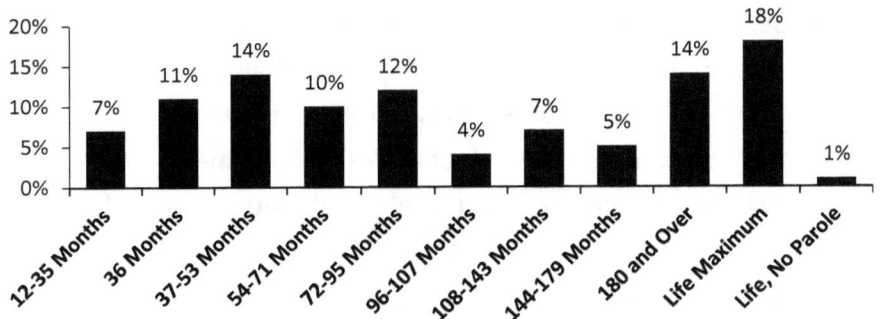

NOVEMBER 24th, 1865

Mississippi Criminalizes Unemployment and Assembly by Free Blacks

Shortly after the end of the Civil War in 1865, Southern states sought to control and confine their large populations of newly-freed black people by passing laws that authorized their arrest and incarceration. These laws, known as "black codes," typically applied only to black people and criminalized acts that were not offenses at all when committed by whites.

In November and December 1865, the Mississippi legislature approved numerous black codes. One passed on November 24, 1865, declared that "all freedmen, free negroes and mulattoes" found without proof of employment or business or found "unlawfully assembling themselves" would be deemed vagrants and, upon conviction, owe up to $50 in fines and serve up to ten days in jail. The same law threatened whites with vagrancy convictions if found assembling or associating with freedmen "on terms of equality" or found "living in adultery" with a black partner. If convicted, whites faced up to $200 in fines and up to six months in jail.

As a result of black codes like these in Mississippi, and similar laws passed during the same period in states throughout the South, the post-Civil War era brought American black people more contact with the criminal court and prison systems than ever before. As the former Confederacy learned to wield the criminal justice system as a tool of racial control, of countless black men, women, and children were convicted and sentenced under unjust laws that criminalized them for existing as free, black citizens.

"Equal Justice Initiative, A History of Racial Injustice Timeline, at http://racialinjustice.eji.org/timeline/1860s/."

NOVEMBER 12th, 1866

Texas Legislature Authorizes Leasing of State Prison Inmates for Profit

Because the Thirteenth Amendment's ban on slavery and involuntary servitude explicitly excepted convicted criminals from its protections, the predominately black populations ensnared by discriminatory criminal laws passed after the Civil War had no way to avoid being thrust back into the conditions of forced labor they had only recently escaped. Soon after the Civil War's end, Texas was one of many states to pass laws making this arrangement possible.

After passing a law authorizing the leasing of jail inmates three days before, the Texas legislature on November 12, 1866, approved a law entitled "An Act to provide for the employment of Convict labor on works of public utility," which empowered the state to employ or lease certain classes of prisoners to build railroads, work in mines, and staff iron foundries. Prisoners convicted of murder, arson, robbery, burglary, perjury, and horses stealing were exempt from the law and were required to serve their time in the state penitentiary as before; in effect, this classification of prisoners ensured that the vast majority of state inmates eligible to be leased were black convicts.

Convict leasing became a very profitable enterprise for Texas and many other Southern states throughout the 19th and into the 20th century. It proved a very dangerous and even deadly system for the black inmates forced to work in inhumane conditions that historian David Oshinsky has described as "worse than slavery."

"Equal Justice Initiative, A History of Racial Injustice Timeline, at http://racialinjustice.eji.org/timeline/1860s/."

MAY 11th, 1868

Convict Leasing Begins in Georgia

After the Civil War, Georgia and other Southern states faced economic uncertainty. Dependent on enslaved black labor that was no longer available after emancipation and ratification of the Thirteenth Amendment, Southern economies struggled to find a new solution. For many, leasing state convicts to labor for private businesses seemed the perfect answer.

Ratified in 1865, the Thirteenth Amendment prohibited involuntary servitude "except as punishment for crime" and seemingly permitted the forced labor of prisoners. At the same time, Southern prison populations had grown greatly following the Civil War, and that increase was disproportionately fueled by newly-emancipated black men and women incarcerated for violating discriminatory Black Codes that criminalized unemployment and vagrancy and severely punished even the most minor thefts.

On May 11, 1868, in the midst of Reconstruction, Georgia Provisional Governor Thomas Ruger leased 100 black prisoners to William A. Fort of the Georgia & Alabama Railroad for one year for $2,500 under an agreement that made Mr. Fort responsible for their well-being. Sixteen prisoners died before the end of the contract. Undeterred, Georgia officials expanded the system the following year, leasing all 393 state prisoners to work on another railroad. Over the next several years, convict leasing in Georgia proved both deadly and profitable. The state legislature routinely turned a blind eye to reports of inhumane treatment and even murder and, in 1876, authorized the state to enter into long-term, twenty-year convict leasing contracts valued at $500,000.

"Equal Justice Initiative, A History of Racial Injustice Timeline, at http://racialinjustice.eji.org/timeline/1860s/."

JULY 28th, 1868

Fourteenth Amendment Is Adopted

On July 28, 1868, Secretary of State William Seward certified the adoption of the Fourteenth Amendment to the United States Constitution. The Fourteenth Amendment grants citizenship to "all persons born or naturalized in the United States," including former black slaves freed as a result of the Emancipation Proclamation and the Thirteenth Amendment. The Fourteenth Amendment also forbids states from denying any person "life, liberty or property, without due process of law" or to "deny to any person within its jurisdiction the equal protection of its laws." By directly mentioning the role of the states, the Fourteenth Amendment notably expanded civil rights protections to black people formerly at the mercy of discriminatory state legislatures.

With the exception of Tennessee, all Southern states refused to ratify the Fourteenth Amendment when it was initially proposed in June 1866. In response to their abstinence, the Republican-controlled Congress passed the Reconstruction Act of 1867, authorizing the establishment of military governments in the Southern states and making ratification of the Fourteenth

Amendment a condition of readmission to the Union. Tennessee, which had already ratified, was exempt from the act's other provisions.

Final ratification of the amendment required approval by three-quarters of the states; after Ohio and New Jersey attempted to rescind their earlier ratifications, the threshold was met with Georgia's ratification on July 21, 1868.

One week later, official CERTIFICATION was announced. Notably, while the Fourteenth Amendment extended citizenship to black Americans, Native Americans would not officially become United States citizens until the passage of the Indian Citizenship Act in 1924.[2]

"Equal Justice Initiative, A History of Racial Injustice Timeline, at http://racialinjustice.eji.org/timeline/1860s/."

(1) Department of Corrections and Community Supervision.
(2) Equal Justice Initiative.

Chapter 5

"Government uses Prison Labor to make Military Uniforms"

The Berry Amendment is a statutory requirement that restricts the Department of Defense (DoD) from using funds appropriated or otherwise available to DoD for procurement of food, clothing, fabrics, fibers, yarns, other made-up textiles, and hand or measuring tools that are not grown, reprocessed, reused, or produced in the United States. The Berry Amendment has been critical to maintaining the safety and security of our armed forces, by requiring covered items to be produced in the United States. With respect to textiles and clothing, the Berry Amendment has been critical to the viability of the textile and clothing production base in the United States.

In World War II-era called the Berry Amendment was to have most of the military uniforms made in the United States. Wages today are under $2 per hour. They have turned to federal prisons for their labor. In 2015 the federal inmates stitched more than $100 million dollars' worth of military uniforms.

All in all nearly a million prisoners are now making office furniture, working in call centers, fabricating body armor, even taking hotel reservations, working in slaughterhouses, or manufacturing textiles, shoes, and clothing, while getting paid somewhere between 93 cents and $4.73 per day.

This criminal justice system is definitely an enigma. Prisons abuse, overpopulated and corruption running widespread throughout private prisons, with even some judges receiving financial incentive to jail individuals, inmate abuse and high numbers of children in solitary confinement.

This lowers the cost of producing their military uniforms and also add to the growing list of other products that prison laborers produces. It provides the cheapest of labor to produce government necessities.

It is common knowledge that prisoners made license plates, but what else are they making in prisons today, that you may use without ever probably without realizing it. For instants, books for the blind, lingerie, park benches and picnic tables, human shaped targets, baseball caps, blue jeans, canoes, and of course military uniforms, these are just a few to name.

With judges receiving financial incentive to jail individuals, inmate abuse, and high numbers of children in solitary confinement. With the government searching for cheap prison labor government scratching the backs of private corporations and therefore, undermining the efforts of legitimate private sector businesses.

Business owners are crying foul over the number of clothing contracts -- including those for military uniforms -- awarded to Federal Prison Industries, also known as UNICOR. Unicorp is a government-run enterprise that employs over 13,000 inmates, paying wages as low as 23 cents per hour, to make goods for the Pentagon and other government agencies.

Unicorp is also known as Federal Prison Industries, and is part of the US Bureau of Prisons. It has been preparing inmates FOR JOBS after they get out of prison since 1934.

Last year it was reported that two Alabama based clothing manufacturer were cutting JOBS by the hundreds, due to not being able to compete with the FPI.

In 1980, when Ronald Reagan became president, there were approximately 400,000 prisoners in prison. Today, the number exceeds 2.3 million. In California the prison population ascended from 23,264 in 1980 to 170,000 in 2010. The Pennsylvania prison population ascended from 8,243 to 51,487 in those same years. There are now more African-American men in prison, on probation or on parole than were enslaved in 1850, before the Civil War began, according to Law Professor Michelle Alexander in the book "The New Jim Crow: Mass Incarceration in the Age of Colorblindness."

The racism that permeates every aspect of life in capitalist society — from jobs, income and housing to education or opportunity — is most brutally reflected by who is caught up in the U.S. prison system. More than 60 percent of U.S. prisoners are non-white. Seventy percent of those being sentenced under the three strikes law in California — which requires mandatory sentences of 25 years to life after three felony convictions — are non-white people. Nationally, 39 percent of African-American men in their 20s are in prison. These are the most productive years for men. This is more than Africa did under apartheid, believe it or not.

Today, an overwhelming 1-in-100 adults in the U.S. are living behind bars. But this is a crime, which breaks families and destroys lives, and is not evenly distributed. In major urban areas one-half of Black men have criminal records. This means life-long, legalized discrimination in student loans, financial assistance, access to public housing, mortgages, the right to vote and of course, the possibility of being hired for a job. This is our prison system today.

Chapter 6

"Incarceration Trends in America"

- From 1980 to 2008, the number of people incarcerated in America quadrupled-from roughly 500,000 to 2.3 million people

- Today, the US is 5% of the World population and has 25% of world prisoners.

- Combining the number of people in prison and jail with those under parole or probation supervision, 1 in ever y 31 adults, or 3.2 percent of the population is under some form of correctional control

Racial Disparities in Incarceration

- African Americans now constitute nearly 1 million of the total 2.3 million incarcerated population

- African Americans are incarcerated at nearly six times the rate of whites

- Together, African American and Hispanics comprised 58% of all prisoners in 2008, even though African Americans and Hispanics make up approximately one quarter of the US population

- According to Unlocking America, if African American and Hispanics were incarcerated at the same rates of whites, today's prison and jail populations would decline by approximately 50%

- One in six black men had been incarcerated as of 2001. If current trends continue, one in three black males born today can expect to spend time in prison during his lifetime

- 1 in 100 African American women are in prison

- Nationwide, African-Americans represent 26% of juvenile arrests, 44% of youth who are detained, 46% of the youth who are judicially waived to criminal court, and 58% of the youth admitted to state prisons (Center on Juvenile and Criminal Justice).

Drug Sentencing Disparities

- About 14 million Whites and 2.6 million African Americans report using an illicit drug

- 5 times as many Whites are using drugs as African Americans, yet African Americans are sent to prison for drug offenses at 10 times the rate of Whites

- African Americans represent 12% of the total population of drug users, but 38% of those arrested for drug offenses, and 59% of those in state prison for a drug offense.

- African Americans serve virtually as much time in prison for a drug offense (58.7 months) as whites do for a violent offense (61.7 months). (Sentencing Project)

Contributing Factors

- Inner city crime prompted by social and economic isolation

- Crime/drug arrest rates: African Americans represent 12% of monthly drug users, but comprise 32% of persons arrested for drug possession

- "Get tough on crime" and "war on drugs" policies

- Mandatory minimum sentencing, especially disparities in sentencing for crack and powder cocaine possession

- In 2002, blacks constituted more than 80% of the people sentenced under the federal crack cocaine laws and served substantially more time in prison for drug offenses than did whites, despite that fact that more than 2/3 of crack cocaine users in the U.S. are white or Hispanic

- "Three Strikes" habitual offender policies

- Zero Tolerance policies as a result of perceived problems of school violence; adverse effect on black children.

- 35% of black children grades 7-12 have been suspended or expelled at some point in their school careers compared to 20% of Hispanics and 15% of whites

Effects of Incarceration

- Jail reduces work time of young people over the next decade by 25-30 percent when compared with arrested youths who were not incarcerated

- Jails and prisons are recognized as settings where society's infectious diseases are highly concentrated

- Prison has not been proven as a rehabilitation for behavior, as two-thirds of prisoners will reoffend

Exorbitant Cost of Incarceration: Is it Worth It?

- About $70 billion dollars are spent on corrections yearly

- Prisons and jails consume a growing portion of the nearly $200 billion we spend annually on public safety

Chapter 7

Strange Math in the Census

I've also learned that The US Census system counts prisoners as residents of the towns where they are imprisoned and not the communities where their homes and families are located. This is monies that will go to the township which the prison is located. In reality, nearly 75% of the inmates in New York State prisons hail from seven neighborhoods in New York City. Bedford-Stuyvesant, Brownsville, East New York, Harlem, Manhattan's Lower East Side, South Bronx, and South Jamaica Queens.

As a New Yorker and as Americans, we need to learn more about both our prisons and our prisoners. I was surprised when I learned what all the prisoners make in prison. I knew this was slave labor written in The 13th Amendment to the Constitution.

The system is arresting our African Black men/women in alarming rates compared to the same crimes the White race commits. This is something that everyone should be outraged about. I don't know how many people really understand the justice system in the US, when it's comes to African Black people. There is no justice for an African Black American men/women living in the United States.

TheRichest – *"10 Products You Didn't Know Were Made By Prisoners"*

As you've probably seen on the Netflix series, Orange is the New Black; prisoners in America do odd jobs while serving their sentences. U.S. inmates in federal and state prisons also provide a unique labor force for the publicly traded corporations in America. From raising and training seeing-eye dogs to operating fully functional call centers, prison labor has permeated every industry of America's capitalist society.

These inmate workers often work for Federal Prison Industries Incorporated (FPI). FPI was established on June 23, 1934 when President Franklin D. Roosevelt signed it into law. FPI was organized as a "state use" system which restricted sales to only the federal government in order to not negatively affect the private sector.

FPI has transformed itself over the years into a mega corporation. In 1974 FPI was organized into seven divisions: automated data processing, electronics, graphics, metals, shoe & brush, textiles and Woods and plastics. 1977 marked FPI's new corporate logo and trade name, UNICOR. New lines were also introduced that included stainless steel products, thermoplastics, printed circuits, modular furniture, ergonomic chairs, and optics. These new lines were created in order to increase UNICOR's competitive position. ACCORDING to CNN in 2011 UNICOR's annual revenue was $900 million. UNICOR has been able to show its effectiveness on REHABILITATING inmates with its seven year study titled the Post-Release Employment Project (PREP). The study compared post-release activities of inmates who had participated in UNICOR to those that did not and the findings showed that those that participated in UNICOR were 24 percent less likely to return to prison than those that did not participate in the program.

Despite the positives of the program for the inmates, the private sector of businesses have been having a hard time being able to keep up with the way UNICOR operates. For example, according to ABC News wages paid to inmate workers are sometime as low as 23 cents and federal law requires government agencies to buy products from UNICOR without competitive bidding. According to The Nation, starting in the 90's many inmates began to be employed by subcontractors in order to provide work at slave rate wages for large for-profit corporations. However, it is often difficult to pinpoint which giant corporations are using inmate labor since they don't want to have any ties with it due to marketing purposes.

Many corporations are hiring prison labor, directly or indirectly as it allows them to be able to cut their own costs since inmates are paid way less than the average worker and they are not offered any type of medical benefits.

Here is a list of products that you probably didn't know were made by prisoners in America.

Solar Panels

The Electronics Business Group produces renewable energy solutions for federal agencies, known in the industry as photovoltaic solar modules, predictable and controlled energy sourcing, and on-site renewable energy supply.

McDonalds Employee Uniforms

McDonalds publicly states their commitment to human rights stating "We do not use any form of slave, forced, bonded, indentured, or involuntary prison labor. However the fast-food giant indirectly uses prison labor by working with subcontractors that provide uniforms that have been sewn by Oregon inmates. The prison labor is voluntary, but one needs to question if prison labor can ever really be "voluntary?"

Military Attire and Battle Gear

UNICOR's inmate employees work on making jackets, helmets, uniforms and shoes for the United States military. An Alabama company, American Apparel Inc. also provides the same services to the U.S. military however, an executive at the company told CNN Money that competition for the contracts has become too stiff resulting in the company having to lay off 150 people over several years.

Packaging Starbucks Coffee Beans

At the Twin Rivers Corrections Unit in Monroe, Washington, Signature Packaging Solutions uses inmate labor for its packaging needs. Signature Packaging Solutions provides packaging services for corporations such as Starbucks. In 2002, Starbucks' public affairs director Audrey Lincoff released a statement to the Seattle Weekly stating "Starbucks is aware that Signature uses inmate labor and believes its contract with Signature is entirely consistent with our mission statement."

Braille Books

In 2001 The National Prison Braille Network (NPBN) began to team up with correctional facilities across the United States and the American Printing House for the Blind (APH) in order to create quality braille textbooks for blind students in grades K-12. As of 2009 there were 31 braille PROGRAMS operating in correctional facilities in 26 states. 29 out of the 31 programs operate in state prisons while two operate under federal facilities. The goal of the prisons who work with the APH is to prepare inmates for reentry into society.

Furniture

ACCORDING to Government Executive, furniture is UNICOR's biggest business with furniture sales making up more than 40 percent of total sales. Back when Clinton was in office, Tipper Gore's side chairs were reupholstered by inmates who work for UNICOR and former Attorney General Janet Reno held meetings over a conference table that had been refinished by UNICOR workers.

Victoria's Secret Lingerie

It was during the 90's that South Carolina inmates were hired by subcontractor, Third Generation Inc. to sew Victoria's Secret lingerie and leisure wear. Third Generation Inc. operated a garment manufacturing plant inside of the Leath Correctional Facility. The Leath plant has produced more than $1.5 million worth of garments.

Law Enforcement Training Gear

Prisoners are often found making human silhouette TARGETS which are used in law enforcement training and Texas prisoners make duty belts, handcuff cases and prison-cell accessories for law enforcement officers.

Packaging of Nintendo Games

During the holiday season, inmates at Twin Rivers Corrections Unit in Washington worked on packaging Nintendo Game Boys and games such as Super Mario Bros. and Donkey Kong. The inmates worked under subcontractor, Signature Packaging Solutions and the inmates stated that the work was very dull and repetitive but at least inmates were paid $6.72 an hour versus their normal RATE of 35 cents to $1.10 an hour.

Circuit Boards

Many tech companies such as IBM, DELL and Texas Instruments have turned to prison labor to make their circuit boards. While these companies do not work directly with prison labor they work with the suppliers that contract out to the prison labor force.

TheRichest – "5 Clothing Brands that are manufactured in Prison"

When you picture prison, you probably imagine scenes of cold steel bars and grey walls, punctuated with the bright orange of jumpsuit-clad men and women. As their sentences bear on, they spend their days toiling away at the gym, playing cards, and maybe smoking the odd cigarette. Between the shapeless, glaring uniforms that they are made to wear and the fact that the majority of prisoners are men, it would seem that prison is the furthest thing away from fashion and that it may be one of the only places where fashion has no place and does not matter.

While the initial image of uniforms, steel, and endless grey may be somewhat accurate, the fact that prisoners are able to sit around all day fantasizing about their release is not. When it comes right down to it, it simply is not economically viable. In America, where the highest incarceration rate in the world exists, there are approximately 2.3 million people in jail. To put this in perspective, this is more than the number of people that live in Houston, Texas; America's fourth largest city. It is also much higher than the number of people in jail in China, a nation that has a population of more than 1 billion people and that does not shy away from disciplinary action either. In the end, these 2.3 million inmates end up costing taxpayers around $63 billion each year.

But someone had an idea. Why not have prisoners work for a small company or a large corporation while in jail? The labour would be cheap and the money spent on keeping that person in jail will be cycled back into the economy via the products they are able to produce. This is how manufacturing in prison was born in the United States and the manufactured goods range from food products to technology, really anything that can be made in a factory, including fashion.

However, the United States is not the only country that does this and economics is not the only reason. In other countries, the manufacturing of products, clothing especially, is seen as part of social reform within the prison system. Many inmates do not have higher educational backgrounds or any employable skills; so by having them participate in the manufacturing of goods, they are gaining job experience that they can take with them when they are released. Whether it is for economic gain or social betterment, here are 5 brands that sell clothing made in prison.

Prison Blues and Correction Connection

Prison Blues was created in 1989 in Oregon with the intention of manufacturing garments to assist in covering the costs of the inmates' stays at the Eastern Oregon Correctional Institute and without damaging local private businesses.

To set up their enterprise, they used a grant given to them by the government that consisted of money retrieved from drug trafficking. In order to participate as a factory employee, inmates must not only demonstrate good behavior but also successfully complete an interviewing process. Once an employee, they must remain productive at all times inside and outside of work. One benefit of being an employee is that they get to keep approximately 20 percent of their earnings, with the other 80 percent being used to cover the cost of their stay and any of their other expenses, such as family support and paying taxes. These positions at Prison Blues are so coveted that there is even a 3-year waiting list. The Correction Connection helps Prison Blues to distribute their product in-store and online, and products range from t-shirts to jeans. Interestingly, they also manufacture uniforms for other prisons in the state of Oregon.

Stripes Clothing

Stripes Clothing was created by four individuals who are not incarcerated but who took a tour of a prison during the final year of their studies. They concluded that in prison, one can easily become detached from the real world, losing the sense that freedom exists and in turn their motivation. "By maintaining work rhythm in prison, the life of a prisoner does not entirely stand still" and they are given access to the normalcy of attending work every day, like everybody else. They also strengthen their social skills, along with the technical skills associated with producing a garment. Stripes Clothing was founded in the Netherlands and four prisons participate in clothing manufacturing there. A prison in France along with the Eastern Oregon Correctional Institute of Prison Blues has also teamed up with Stripes Clothing.

Haeftling

When German jails first started wanting to sell their clothes, they were uneasy about stating where they were made. Surely they thought that judgment would be passed and that people may not want them due to negative connotations. However, one businessman named Stephan Bohle decided that it was nothing to be feared and boldly named the label Haeftling, German for "jailbird". Since then, the brand has never looked back and they have sold garments to people from Germany to Australia to Japan. They have in fact been so successful that they expanded into leather briefcases, bed linens, and even a specialty line of schnapps.

JCPenney

As a department store, JCPenney sells a variety of items from appliances to baby clothes, all made by various companies representing different brands. They also have their own brand, called jcp. Between all of these, prison labour has come into play. Though they state on a government labour website that they do not knowingly outsource their manufacturing to foreign companies that use prison labour, it really says nothing about working with companies that employ inmates in their own country, which is interesting. Though perhaps they have ceased buying from companies that produce their garments in US prisons, many sources state that it is their lingerie that is made by inmates, which brings us to our next brand.

Victoria's Secret

This one is probably the most bizarre and maybe even a little disturbing to some consumers on a variety of levels. Not only is it quite odd to picture your stereotypical balding, tattooed prisoner handling your soon-to-be unmentionables, it also may be a little disconcerting that this company, like JCPenney, is a large, successful retailer that doesn't really need to be saving money by producing their products in prison. Unlike the first three projects mentioned, Victoria's Secret manufacturing some of their goods in prison is not simply for the good of the inmates, but it also directly benefits Victoria's Secret. This has led to some controversy about whether it is ethical to be employing inmates where it is beneficial to not just the inmate and the taxpayer, but also to this new third party, the corporation. Regardless, it still provides inmates with something constructive to do each day and with some skills to take with them when they are released, so it would seem that everybody wins. Now I wonder if they'll accept employee transfers ... Probably not.

Chapter 8

WORLD

"21st-Century Slaves: How Corporations Exploit Prison Labor"

In the eyes of the corporation, inmate labor is a brilliant strategy in the eternal quest to maximize profit.

Rania Khalek, AlterNet, July 21, 2011

There is one group of American workers so disenfranchised that corporations are able to get away with paying them wages that rival those of third-world sweatshops. These laborers have been legally stripped of their political, economic and social rights and ultimately relegated to second-class citizens. They are banned from unionizing, violently silenced from speaking out and forced to work for little to no wages. This marginalization renders them practically invisible, as they are kept hidden from society with no AVAILABLE recourse to improve their circumstances or change their plight.

They are the 2.3 million American prisoners locked behind bars where we cannot see or hear them. And they are modern-day slaves of the 21st century.

Incarceration Nation

It's no secret that AMERICA imprisons more of its citizens than any other nation in history. With just 5 percent of the world's population, the US currently holds 25 percent of the world's prisoners. "In 2008, over 2.3 million Americans were in prison or jail, with one of every 48 working-age men behind bars," according to a study by the Center for Economic and Policy Research (CEPR).

That doesn't include the tens of thousands of detained undocumented immigrants facing deportation, prisoners awaiting sentencing, or juveniles caught up in the school-to-prison pipeline. Perhaps it's reassuring to some that the US still holds the NUMBER one title in at least one arena, but needless to say the hyper-incarceration plaguing America has had a damaging effect on society at large.

The CEPR study observes that US prison rates are not just excessive in comparison to the rest of the world, they are also "substantially higher than our own longstanding history." The STUDY finds that incarceration rates between 1880 and 1970 ranged from about "100 to 200 prisoners per 100,000 people." After 1980, the INMATE population "began to grow much more rapidly than the overall population and the RATE climbed from" about 220 in 1980 to 458 in 1990, 683 in 2000, and 753 in 2008."

The costs of this incarceration industry are far from evenly distributed, with the impact of excessive incarceration falling predominantly on African-American communities. Although black people make up just 13 percent of the overall population, they ACCOUNT for 40 percent of US prisoners. According to the Bureau of Justice Statistics (BJS), black males are incarcerated at a rate "more than 6.5 times that of white males and 2.5 that of Hispanic males and "black females are incarcerated at approximately three times the rate of white females and twice that of Hispanic females."

Michelle Alexander points out in her book The New Jim Crow that more black men "are in prison or jail, on probation or on parole than were enslaved in 1850." Higher rates of black drug arrests do not reflect higher rates of black drug offenses. In fact, whites and blacks engage in drug offenses, possession and sales at roughly comparable rates.

Incentivizing Incarceration

Clearly, the US prison system is riddled with racism and classism, but it gets worse. As it turns out, private companies have a cheap, easy labor market, and it isn't in China, Indonesia, Haiti, or Mexico. It's right here in the land of the free, where large corporations increasingly employ prisoners as a source of cheap and sometimes free labor.

In the eyes of the corporation, inmate labor is a brilliant strategy in the eternal quest to maximize profit. By dipping into the prison labor pool, companies have their pick of workers who are not only cheap but easily controlled. Companies are free to avoid providing benefits like health insurance or sick days, while simultaneously paying little to no wages. They don't need to worry about unions or demands for vacation time or raises. Inmates work full-time and are never late or absent because of family problems.

"If they refuse to work, they are moved to disciplinary housing and lose canteen privileges" along with "good time credit that reduces their sentences," reports Chris Levister. To top it off, Abe Louise Young reports in The Nation that the federal government subsidizes the use of inmate labor by private companies through lucrative tax write-offs. Under the Work Opportunity Tax Credit (WOTC), private-sector employers receive a tax credit of $2,400 for every work release inmate they employ as a reward for hiring "risky target groups" and they can "earn back up to 40 percent of the wages they pay annually to target group workers."

Study after study demonstrates the wastefulness of America's prison-industrial complex, in both taxpayer dollars and innocent lives, yet rolling back imprisonment rates is proving to be more challenging than ever. Meanwhile, the use of private prisons and now privately contracted inmate labor has created a system that does not exactly incentivize leaner sentencing.

The disturbing implications of such a system mean that skyrocketing imprisonment for the possession of miniscule amounts of marijuana and the expansion of severe mandatory sentencing laws regardless of the conviction, are policies that have the potential to increase corporate profits. As are the "three strikes laws" that require courts to hand down mandatory and extended sentences to people who have been convicted of felonies on three or more separate occasions. People have literally been sentenced to life for minor crimes like shoplifting.

The Reinvention of Slavery

The exploitation of prison labor is by no means a new phenomenon. Jaron Browne, an organizer with People Organized to Win Employment Rights (POWER), maps out how the exploitation of prison labor in America is rooted in slavery. The abolition of slavery dealt a devastating economic blow to the South following the loss of free labor after the Civil War. So in the late 19th century, "an extensive prison system was created in the South in order to maintain the racial and economic relationship of slavery," a mechanism responsible for re-enslaving black workers. Browne describes Louisiana's famous Angola Prison to illustrate the intentional transformation from slave to inmate:

"In 1880, this 8000-acre family plantation was purchased by the state of Louisiana and converted into a prison. Slave quarters became cell units. Now expanded to 18,000 acres, the Angola plantation is tilled by prisoners working the land—a chilling picture of modern day chattel slavery."

The abolition of slavery quickly gave rise to the Black Codes and Convict Leasing, which together worked wonders at perpetuating African American servitude by exploiting a loophole in the 13th Amendment to the US Constitution.

The Black Codes were a set of laws that "criminalized legal activity for African Americans" and provided a pretext for the arrest and mass imprisonment of newly freed blacks, which caused the rate of African Americans prisoners to "surpass whites for the first time", according to Randall G. Sheldon in the Black Commentator. Convict leasing involved leasing out prisoners to private companies that paid the state a certain fee in return. Convicts worked for the companies during the day outside the prison and returned to their cells at night. The system provided revenue for the state and profits for plantation owners and wasn't abolished until the 1930s.

Unfortunately, convict leasing was quickly replaced with equally despicable state-run chain gangs. Once again, stories of vicious abuse created enough public anger to abolish chain gangs by the 1950s. Nevertheless, the systems of prisoner exploitation never actually disappeared.

Today's corporations can lease factories in prisons, as well as lease prisoners out to their factories. In many cases, private corporations are running prisons-for-profit, further incentivizing their stake in locking people up. The government is profiting as well, by running prison factories that operate as "multibillion-dollar industries in every state, and throughout the federal prison system," where prisoners are contracted out to major corporations by the state.

In the most extreme cases, we are even witnessing the re-emergence of the chain gang. In Arizona, the self-proclaimed "toughest sheriff in America," Joe Arpaio, requires his Maricopa County inmates to enroll in chain gangs to perform various community services or face lockdown with three other inmates in an 8-by-12-foot cell, for 23 hours a day. In June of this year, Arpaio started a female-only chain gang made up of women convicted of driving under the influence. In a press release he boasted that the inmates would be wearing pink T-shirts emblazoned with messages about drinking and driving.

The modern-day version of convict leasing was recently spotted in Georgia, where Governor Nathan Deal proposed sending unemployed probationers to work in Georgia's fields as a solution to a perceived labor shortage following the passage of the country's most draconian anti-immigrant law. But his plan backfired when some of the probationers began walking off their jobs because the fieldwork was too strenuous.

There has also been a disturbing re-emergence of the debtors' prison, which should serve as an ominous sign of our dangerous reliance on prisons to manage any and all of society's problems. According to the Wall Street Journal, "more than a third of all U.S. states allow borrowers who can't or won't pay to be jailed." They found that judges "signed off on more than 5,000 such warrants since the start of 2010 in nine counties." It appears that any act that can be criminalized in the era of private prisons and inmate labor will certainly end in jail time, further increasing the ranks of the captive workforce.

Who Profits?

Prior to the 1970s, private corporations were prohibited from using prison labor as a result of the chain gang and convict leasing scandals. But in 1979, the US Department of Justice admits that congress began a process of deregulation to "restore private sector involvement in prison industries to its former status, provided certain conditions of the labor market were met." Over the last 30 years, at least 37 states have enacted laws permitting the use of convict labor by private enterprise, with an average pay of $0.93 to $4.73 per day.

Federal prisoners receive more generous wages that range from $0.23 to $1.25 per hour, and are employed by Unicor, a wholly owned government corporation established by Congress in 1934. Its principal customer is the Department of Defense, from which Unicor derives approximately 53 percent of its sales. Some 21,836 inmates work in Unicor programs. Subsequently, the nation's prison industry – prison labor programs producing goods or services sold to other government agencies or to the private sector -- now employs more people than any Fortune 500 company (besides General Motors), and generates about $2.4 billion in revenue annually. Noah Zatz of UCLA law school estimates that:

"Well over 600,000, and probably close to a million, inmates are working full-time in jails and prisons throughout the United States. Perhaps some of them built your desk chair: office furniture, especially in state universities and the federal government, is a major prison labor product. Inmates also take hotel reservations at corporate call centers, make body armor for the U.S. military, and manufacture prison chic fashion accessories, in addition to the iconic task of stamping license plates."

Some of the largest and most powerful corporations have a stake in the expansion of the prison labor market, including but not limited to IBM, Boeing, Motorola, Microsoft, AT&T, Wireless, Texas Instrument, Dell, Compaq, Honeywell, Hewlett-Packard, Nortel, Lucent Technologies, 3Com, Intel, Northern Telecom, TWA, Nordstrom's, Revlon, Macy's, Pierre Cardin, Target Stores, and many more. Between 1980 and 1994 alone, profits went up from $392 million to $1.31 billion. Since the prison labor force has likely grown since then, it is safe to assume that the profits accrued from the use of prison labor have reached even higher levels.

In an article for Mother Jones, Caroline Winter details a number of mega-corporations that have profited off of inmates:

"In the 1990s, subcontractor Third Generation hired 35 female South Carolina inmates to sew lingerie and leisure wear for Victoria's Secret and JCPenney. In 1997, a California prison put two men in solitary for telling journalists they were ordered to replace 'Made in Honduras' labels on garments with "Made in the USA."

According to Winter, the defense industry is a large part of the equation as well:

"Unicor, says that in addition to soldiers' uniforms, bedding, shoes, helmets, and flak vests, inmates have 'produced missile cables (including those used on the Patriot missiles during the Gulf War)' and 'wiring harnesses for jets and tanks.' In 1997, according to Prison Legal News, Boeing subcontractor MicroJet had prisoners cutting airplane components, paying $7 an hour for work that paid union wages of $30 on the outside."

Oil companies have been known to exploit prison labor as well. Following the explosion of the Deepwater Horizon rig that killed 11 workers and irreparably damaged the Gulf of Mexico for generations to come, BP elected to hire Louisiana prison inmates to clean up its mess. Louisiana has the highest incarceration rate of any state in the nation, 70 percent of which are African-American men. Coastal residents desperate for work, whose livelihoods had been destroyed by BP's negligence, were outraged at BP's use of free prison labor.

In the Nation article that exposed BP's hiring of inmates, Abe Louise Young details how BP tried to cover up its use of prisoners by changing the inmates' clothing to give the illusion of civilian workers. But nine out of 10 residents of Grand Isle, Louisiana are white, while the cleanup workers were almost exclusively black, so BP's ruse fooled very few people.

Private companies have long understood that prison labor can be as profitable as sweatshop workers in third-world countries with the added benefit of staying closer to home. Take Escod Industries, which in the 1990s abandoned plans to open operations in Mexico and instead "moved to South Carolina, because the wages of American prisoners undercut those of de-unionized Mexican sweatshop workers," reports Josh Levine in a 1999 article that appeared in Perpective Magazine. The move was fueled by the state, which gave a $250,000 "equipment subsidy" to Escod along with industrial space at below-market rent. Other examples listed by Gordon Lafer in the American Prospect include Ohio's Honda supplier, which "pays its prison workers $2 an hour for the same work for which the UAW has fought for decades to be paid $20 to $30 an hour. Konica, which has hired prisoners to repair its copiers for less than 50 cents an hour. And in Oregon, where private companies can "lease" prisoners at a bargain price of $3 a day."

Even politicians have been known to tap into prison labor for their own personal use. In 1994, a contractor for GOP congressional candidate Jack Metcalf hired Washington state prisoners to call and remind voters he was pro-death penalty. After WINNING his campaign, he claimed to have no knowledge of the scandal. Perhaps this is why Senator John Ensign (R-NV) introduced a bill earlier this year to "require all low-security prisoners to work 50 hours a week." After all, The New York Times reminds us that "creating a national prison labor force has been a goal of his since he went to Congress in 1995."

In an unsettling turn of EVENTS lawmakers have begun ditching public employees in favor of free prison labor. The New York Times recently REPORTED that states are "enlisting prison labor to close budget gaps" to offset cuts in "federal financing and dwindling tax revenue." At a time of record UNEMPLOYMENT, inmates are being hired to "paint vehicles, clean courthouses, sweep campsites and perform many other services done before the recession by private contractors or government employees." In Wisconsin, prisoners are now taking up JOBS that were once held by unionized workers, as a result of Governor Scott Walker's contentious anti-union law.

Why You Should Care

Those who argue in favor of prison labor claim it is a useful tool for REHABILITATION and preparation for post-jail employment. But this has only been shown to be true in cases where prisoners are exposed to meaningful employment, where they learn new skills, not the labor-intensive, menial and often dangerous work they are being tasked with. While little if any evidence exists to suggests that the current prison labor system decreases recidivism or leads to better employment prospects outside of prison, there are a number of solutions that have been proven to be useful.

ACCORDING to a study by the Pew Charitable Trusts, "having a history of incarceration itself impedes subsequent economic success." Pew found that "past incarceration reduced subsequent wages by 11 percent, cut annual employment by nine weeks and reduced yearly earnings by 40 percent." The study suggests that the best approach is for state and federal authorities to "invest in PROGRAMS that reconnect inmates to the labor market," as well as "provide training and job placement services around the time of release." Most importantly, Pew suggests that in the long term, America must move toward alternative sentencing programs for low-level and nonviolent offenders, and issuing penalties that are actually proportionate with real public safety concerns.

The exploitation of any workforce is detrimental to all workers. Cheap and FREE labor pushes down wages for everyone. Just as American workers cannot compete with sweatshop labor, the same goes for prison labor. Many jobs that come into prison are taken from free citizens. The American labor movement must demand that prison labor be allowed the right to unionize, the right to a fair and living wage, and the right to a safe and healthy work environment. That is what prisoners are demanding, but they can only do so much from inside a prison cell.

As UNEMPLOYMENT on the outside increases, so too will crime and incarceration rates, and our 21st-century version of corporate slavery will continue to expand unless we do something about it.

Chapter 9

"Companies That Get Rich off Prisoners"

There are approximately 2.4 million people in the United States in prisons today. This number has grown by 700% in the past 30 years. While the United States has only 5% of the world's population it even beats out China with four times the population rate. The United States holds 25 percent of the world's total prisoners. In 2013, one in every 108 adults was in prison or in jail or probation, and one in every 28 children in America had at least one parent if not both behind bars.

Why do think that we have so many people in prison today?

Well revenue is the main reason, so many people are in prisons.

Several corporations make huge profits off prisons today. This is by no means going to stop because of the profit. The average cost of a prisoner is around $24,000 to maintain a state prisoner for a year. For them to save money, states that are strapped for cash (USA taxpayers) pay companies to have to deal with their state prisoners. Companies MAKE LARGE REVENUE by running prisons very cheaply as possible and pressing the prisoners and their families for money for basic fess and necessities. As a result of this, private prisons are approximately $70 billion industry today.

You wouldn't believe that about 65 percent of private prison contracts requires a guarantee occupancy. This means states must maintain a certain volume of prisoners -- usually between 85 and 90 percent of occupancy -- or pay companies for vacant beds. Speaking about depraved incentives -- a state tosses money away if it does not have enough prisoners.

Companies and industries making Profits off Prisoners

1. Law Enforcement (Asset Forfeiture)

Asset forfeiture asset seizure is a form of confiscation of assets by the state. It typically applies to the alleged proceeds or instruments of a crime committed. This applies, but is not limited, to terrorist activities, drug related crimes, and other criminal and even civil offenses. Even when the crime was not committed, by the property owner.

When arresting drug dealers, the police can seize cars so they won't be used for other crimes. It can also be unfair because the car doesn't have to belong to the person caught committing a crime. The owner of the vehicle will also be punished even if not having anything to do with the crime.

Law enforcement can take advantage of asset forfeiture because by seizing assets that have been used in a crime. Police officers doesn't have to prove anything, they don't have to prove a crime was even committed.

The property doesn't have to be returned, even when no proven crime was committed. The fees to recover any property is so high that after it has been proven there was no crime, some owners cannot afford to pay fees associated with retrieving they property, so they let it go. So police officials have a large incentive to want to seize assets they believe was used in a crime. They get to keep the assets, this is something they can include in their budget (asset forfeiture).

There is no punishment for seizing asset that of innocent citizens. With stop and frisk in full force they can be stopped and have their assets taking away from them. All Officers have to say is that we think you just committed a crime. A New York reporter did a piece on Tenaha, Texas drives who haven't committed a crime are routinely forced to surrender their cash or cars during routine traffic stops.

Before Eric Holder the Attorney General left office, he announced that the federal government will no longer participate in civil asset forfeiture. This announcement will probably only affect about six percent of asset forfeitures in the United States.

2. Global Tel-Link

Veritas Technologies Corporation and Goldman Sachs purchased Global Tel*Link in 2009 for $345 million. That's a $655 million return on their investment in two years. Exorbitant calling rates make the prison telephone industry one of the most lucrative businesses in the United States today. This industry is so profitable because prison phone companies have state-sanctioned monopolistic control over the state prison markets.

Globel Tel-Link provides about 57 percent of state prisoner's telephone services. Their rates are extremely overpriced. They charge around $17 for a 15-minute phone call. For example, a fifteen minute long-distance phone call from Global Tel*Link costs $2.36 in Massachusetts, but that same call costs more than $17 in Georgia (although the FCC recently voted to limit rates to 25 cents per call for interstate calls). The only options prisoner's families' have is to pay the rate or not speak to their respected love ones.

With the excessive calling rates this makes the prison telephone company one of the most lucrative business in the United States today. The industry is very profitable because prison companies have state-sanctioned monopolistic control over the state prison market.

The link between family contact during incarceration and reduced recidivism is well-documented because studies have found that prisoners who are able to maintain a close connection with family and friends are not as likely to commit crimes once released. On the other hand prisoners who don't have close connections are more likely to end up back in prison after being released.

Prisons said they have high rates due to the need to keep the lines secure and to monitor the calls. This is hard to believe when a few companies hold a vital monopoly on the service and even pay the state a profit based charge. It is up to the state to hire these phone companies. The state itself is MAKING MONEY off these phone calls, do you think they are interested in negotiating a price that is fair, these cost-effective phone plans for their prisoners?

3. Corizon Medical Services

Who and what is Corizon healthcare services? Corizon have approximately 107 clients at 531 facilities across the country serving over 345,000 inmates in 27 states. Corizon Corporate headquarters is located in Brentwood, Tenn. They are the leading provider for correctional healthcare services in the United States.

This is a private for-profit health care service, which we understand their goal is to always maximize their profits which means cutting costs as all private companies do. They provide very low quality of care to their patients. Corizon has recently lost the contract with the care of prisoners at New York City's Rikers Island. They have 114 contracts now, which they are the largest entity in the nation that does this type of service.

The privately held company has come under fire for putting profits ahead of quality care. They have also been sued for using licensed practical nurses to do the jobs that registered nurses are supposed to do. This alone puts patients in danger of receiving inadequate care, this saves Corizon around 35 percent each in nurse's salary. Habitually this will automatically make higher profits for Corizon. It is my understanding that Corizon denies prisoners drugs and proper health care.

They also maintain unsanitary practices, they refuse to transfer prisoners to hospitals when necessary, like many of health care facilities provides inadequate mental health screening and care for prisoners with mental illnesses-- just to mention a few, of the many, patterns. In the past five years, Corizon has been sued 660 times for causing deaths and permanent injuries to prisoners in their care. Nearly half of those cases remain open. Of those that are closed, 91 one in four ended with confidential settlements that Corizon decline to discuss.

4. The Bail & Bond Industry

What happens when people are arrested and arraigned? It can literally take weeks and sometimes months until a trial date is set. This is the most used options that judges use and the most options that judges have to incentivize defendants to return to court for their trials. When the defendant can't afford to post bail, they must either use a bail bond service or stay in jail to await their trial.

Can you believe that America and the Philippines are the only two countries in the world that uses the bail bond system? In other countries, bail bond is considered illegal because they see it as tampering with the justice system.

In order to create a financial incentive to return to court voluntarily, courts routinely ask for bail money commensurate with the seriousness of the charges. A person charged with murder, for example, may be given a US$500,000 bail, meaning the person is liable for the total amount if he or she fails to appear in court.

Most people cannot afford the total amount of bail, so they or their families must contract with a specialist called a bondsman to arrange for bail bonds.

Bail bonds are surety bonds used to guarantee the entire bail amount if the accused party fails to maintain the terms of his or her release. A bail bondsman generally pays the court a large 'blanket bond' to cover multiple clients, then charges each client 10% of his or her total bail figure as a cash guarantee. These cash bonds are considered bail bonds and are generally non-refundable if obtained through bail bondsmen. The main benefit to the client is not having to spend all of his or her time in an unpleasant cell until the trial date.

Bail bonds can be obtained in most areas of the United States 24 hours a day, 7 days a week. Bail bondsmen generally stay available on an 'on call' basis whenever they are away from their offices. The concept of bail bonds for the release of jailed individuals is generally limited to the United States. Many other countries have other methods for creating financial or moral incentives for accused parties to appear in court. Because a number of people intentionally skip town after posting bail bonds, there is also a need for a unique occupation called a bounty hunter. Private individuals can be hired by bail bondsmen to track down and return those clients who fail to appear in court.

Because bail bonds issued by private bail bonding agencies can be non-refundable and excessively expensive, many court systems have created an alternative for accused people and their families. In lieu of the entire bail amount, a 10% cash bond can also be accepted by the court directly. This is the same situation which created the need for bail bondsmen in the first place, but families with the means to generate cash no longer have to go through an intermediary. In essence, bail bondsmen work much like other short-term, high-interest lending institutions. The repayment terms can be brutal.

Bail companies also lobby for laws that encourage or try to force judges to set bail more than any other option. These bail amounts have climbed over the years, and bail bonds are used in around 40 percent of most felony cases.

Those in the bail industry say that this allows the government to take the costs of pre-trial services off of the taxpayers, and put it on to private companies. Critics of the system say that not only does it mean that rich citizens spend less time in jail than poor ones, it is also overused and abused.

Several states have already banned the practice of bail bonds, and more may follow in the future. The financial disadvantages to the accused and his or her family seem to outweigh the potential benefits of release until trial. The 10% cash bond option issued by the court is refundable as long as the accused appears in court without incident. Bail bonds issued by private companies may have even more stringent conditions, since the bail bondsman would be held financially responsible for the entire bail amount if clients should fail to appear.

5. & 6. Aramark Holdings Corp. & Aramark Correctional Services

Aramark Holdings Corp – Is a Philadelphia based company, this is a $15 billion global provider of award-winning services in food, facilities management, and uniforms. Last year Aramark reported their full-year fiscal 2014 results with strong sales and profit growth and provided an initial outlook for fiscal 2015. Additionally, the Board of Directors has approved a 15% increase in the company's regular quarterly dividends.

Aramark Correctional Services – Aramark Holdings Corp., a Philadelphia-based company that contracts through Aramark Correctional Services to provide food to 600 correctional institutions across the United States, was acquired in 2007 for $8.3 billion by investors that included Goldman Sachs.

Aramark, Philadelphia, Pennsylvania

Jul 14, 2015 azdailysun.com

"Michigan ends prison food contract year after company fined"

LANSING, Mich. (AP) — Michigan has terminated a three-year, $145 million contract with Aramark Correctional Services a year after the company hired to feed state prisoners came under scrutiny for unapproved menu substitutions, worker misconduct and other issues, state officials announced Monday.

Gov. Rick Snyder's administration said the state and company mutually agreed to end their relationship 14 ½ months early after being unable to resolve Aramark-initiated talks about contract revisions related to billing and menus. Michigan fined Aramark $200,000 last year for unauthorized food changes, inadequate staffing and employee misconduct such as fraternizing with inmates and drug smuggling.

There also have been maggot problems, though Aramark was cleared of responsibility for incidents in 2014. An Aramark kitchen worker was fired for ordering cake that appeared to have been nibbled by rodents to be served to prisoners. Snyder previously defended sticking with Philadelphia-based Aramark, saying Michigan was on pace to save $14 million a year through privatization.

Trinity Services Group, based in Oldsmar, Florida, will transition to becoming Michigan's new vendor in the next two months under a three-year, $158 million contract up for approval by a state board.

The company was the only other qualified bidder when Michigan first privatized prison food services. "Their business is correctional food service, and they have a proven track record across the country working in other facilities — some 44 states," state Corrections Department Director Heidi Washington said. Aramark has food contracts with schools, colleges, hospitals and stadiums in addition to janitorial and uniform businesses.

Michigan's contract with Aramark was supposed to run through September 2016. Democrats and a liberal advocacy group, while pleased with the contract's cancellation, said the state should no longer bid out prison food services.

The 2013 outsourcing led to the loss of 370 unionized state jobs replaced by lower-paid private workers. "It's plainly obvious now that cutting corners to save money on prison services not only doesn't work, but puts prison guards and families living near prisons at risk," House Minority Leader Tim Greimel said. Snyder, however, said Michigan will see "significant" savings — at least $11.5 million a year — by still having a private firm prepare food in its 33 prisons. In a statement, Aramark said it was disappointed the deal didn't work out, but was proud to serve Michigan "during a major groundbreaking shift to privatization and delivering on our commitments to serve 65 million meals in MDOC facilities and save Michigan taxpayers more than $25 million."

Aramark, which on its website says it has retained 97 percent of its correctional facility business in more than 35 years, said it takes "full responsibility" for its performance in Michigan prisons "while operating in a highly charged political environment that included repeated false claims."

The Snyder administration hired Aramark to prepare food for the Michigan's 43,000 prisoners after initially saying the move would not save enough money. Once Republican lawmakers objected, the administration reversed course, saying mistakes were made in evaluating bidders' proposals. Ohio recently renewed a contract with Aramark to feed 50,000 prison inmates. The company had faced criticism in that state last year over understaffing, running out of food and a few cases of maggots near food prep areas.

Chapter 10

"The Cost(s) of Incarceration"

Steve Rempe, October 24, 2013

Rikers Island – one of the most expensive addresses in all of New York City. Park Avenue. Soho. Chelsea. Midtown.

When one thinks of exclusive ADDRESSES in New York City, the first thing that likely comes to mind is a penthouse overlooking Central Park, or perhaps an historic brownstone in a trendy part of town. But when it comes to expensive living quarters, those addresses have nothing on the more spartan surroundings in the middle of the East River.

A recent study performed by the Independent Budget Office in New York City reveals the staggering amount being spent to house INMATES our nation's largest city. According to the report, the annual cost per inmate in state-run facilities for the year 2012 was an amazing $167,731. That equates to roughly $460 a day, or nearly $14,000 a month.

Even in a city with a cost of living as high as New York's, one is most certain to find significantly better accommodations at a mere fraction of the cost.

To look at it another way, for the annual amount spent to house prisoners in New York City, those same prisoners could attend an Ivy League school – for four years.

Despite attempts to make the prison system more efficient, and despite a reduction in the overall prison population in recent years, the cost per INMATE in New York City has skyrocketed. In 2001, the annual cost per inmate was roughly 122,155, when adjusted for inflation. In a little over a decade, these costs increased over $45,000 per inmate per year.

"Have you seen a lot of outcry on this?" asks former CORRECTION commissioner Martin Horn. "Why doesn't anything happen? Because nobody cares."

"That's why we have Rikers Island," he concludes. "We want these guys out of public view."

But placing inmates out of sight and out of mind doesn't solve the problem. To do so is mere whistling past the graveyard – an ignoring of the inevitable.

When it comes to ASSESSING the total cost of the CORRECTIONS system in the United States, government expenditures are just a part of the equation. There is the lost opportunity cost incurred when potential workers are removed from the economy. There is the additional cost to support children and other family members who are no longer supported by those behind bars. Perhaps most of all, there's the fact that the incarceration itself is doing little to stem the tide of crime, and that those who are being jailed now at these exorbitant costs are likely to return to prison (and most likely an even higher cost) sometime in the future.

To think about simply reducing costs of incarceration is to put the cart in front of the horse. The first priority must be a complete review of the system itself, and how we as a nation approach corrections. Only by examining what it is that leads to astronomical rates of imprisonment, and what is effective in reducing those rates, will we be able to develop a system that is both efficient and effective.

To that end, Justice Fellowship is working to bring about needed reforms to the criminal justice system. Through lobbying efforts on both the state and federal level, Justice Fellowship seeks reforms in sentencing, in-prison policy, and reentry practices that will reduce recidivism rates, lower prison populations, and, ultimately, lower the costs of corrections – both in terms of money paid by government, as well as the costs incurred by families and communities. To learn more about the work Justice Fellowship is doing, and how you can be a part of it, visit www.justicefellowship.org.

44180 Riverside Parkway
Lansdowne VA, 20176
703.554.8607

justicefellowship@pfm.org
press@justicefellowship.org

Average Cost Per Inmate

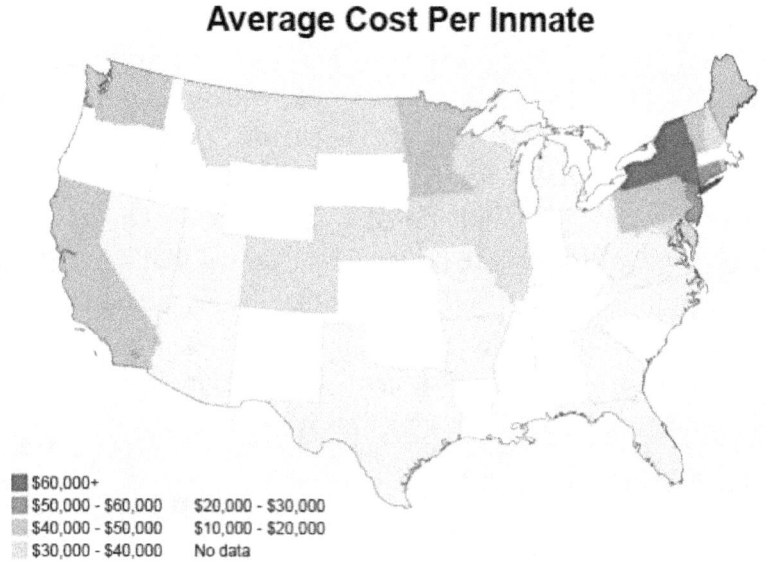

$60,000+
$50,000 - $60,000 $20,000 - $30,000
$40,000 - $50,000 $10,000 - $20,000
$30,000 - $40,000   No data

Chapter 11

"New York State Special Commission"

The Evolution of the New York Prison System [Part I]

The modern prison is truly a legacy from the past. Born out of nineteenth-century reform idealism, the fortress-like penitentiary has weathered shifts in penology and remains a place where the time-honored goal is custody.

The history of the New York prison system clearly shows the development of the American penitentiary. At each point when new approaches have been proposed, the prison itself has prevailed. Many will argue that incarceration has failed because it is built on false assumptions. Others maintain that the problem is a lack of resources and the inadequacies of the prison bureaucracy. As the Attica Commission's report shows, the debate about the purpose and effectiveness of corrections continues.

The American prison system as we know it began in New York in the early 19th century. The founders of this system were men of high purpose, who conceived of prisons as more than simple warehouses of convicted criminals. "Reformation" was their goal, and, as rational men, they developed a concept of imprisonment which was consistent with their beliefs concerning the causes of crime in the simple society of that time. The prisons which these reformers built almost 150 years ago to put their theories into practice survive physically throughout the country and conceptually in maximum security prisons like Attica. [1]

During the colonial period of our history and in the early years of the nation, long-term imprisonment was not a common **form** of punishment. Execution was the prescribed penalty for a wide range of offenses, while the less serious **offenders** faced public punishment, such as pillorying, whipping, and even maiming.

Places for long confinement of convicted offenders were simply not necessary. Commonly called the age of enlightenment, the 18th century was one of dramatic challenge to traditional thought and customs, including concepts of punishment. By the beginning of the 19th century, imprisonment had replaced public punishment and execution for most crimes except murder and treason.

The early places of imprisonment ranged from large wood frame houses in the cities, from which escapes were frequent, to an abandoned copper mine which Connecticut adopted as its prison in 1790. The sole objective of those places of confinement was detention. Imprisonment was its own end, and no pretense was made of rehabilitation. Indeed, long-term confinement was itself considered a progressive, humane improvement over the old system of whipping and execution.

Repulsion from the gallows rather than any faith in the penitentiary spurred the late eighteenth century construction. Few people had any clear idea what the structure should look like or how they should be administered. . . [2]

In the early 19th century, however, two very definite concepts of imprisonment were introduced in New York and Pennsylvania, including what the structures should look like and how they should be operated. These concepts resulted in the construction of entire institutions intended not only to house convicted criminals, but also to reform them into temperate, industrious, hard-working citizens, and to return them to their societies as new men. With the emphasis upon reformation of the criminal, sentences would be long enough to allow the prison program to have its desired effect.

It was no accident that in Pennsylvania the institution was called a penitentiary, for the inmates were there to do penance. The Pennsylvania authorities, reflecting their deeply moralistic Quaker faith, were convinced that man became a lawbreaker through evil influences and corrupt companions.

The key to reforming him lay in separating him from all potential for such wicked association and providing him with a small room and exercise area, totally isolated from the human companionship which had led him astray.

After an appropriate period of total isolation and inactivity, he would be allowed small bits of handicraft work and a Bible in his cell. From the Bible and his work, he would learn the superiority of the life of simple faith, diligent toil, and moderate habits.

Blindfolded upon arrival, he was led to his cell where the blindfold was removed and he remained in his cell until he was released, when he was blindfolded again and led out. The solitary cell and its small exercise yard became his entire world. He never saw another inmate, for even the most fleeting of contacts was considered corrupting. Only in the purity of complete isolation could the corruption be overcome and the restoration of faith and honesty is attained. And in complete isolation he was kept.

The New York authorities preceded on much the same premise as to the cause of crime, but adopted a slightly different solution in the construction of Auburn State Prison in the early 19th century (1819). New Yorkers felt that the isolation of prisoners from arrival to release was too inhuman, it was both unnatural and cruel. Far from reforming men, they felt such absolute solitude bred insanity and despair. In addition, there was the issue, perhaps more pressing, of expense to the state. Inmates restricted to their cells 24 hours a day contributed nothing to the cost of their own confinement. The state had to provide all food, clothing, supplies, and materials to its prisoners.

If the prisoners were to learn the advantages and satisfaction of hard work and thrift, the New York authorities believed, there could be no better way than to be compelled to work together in harmony, if such a system also offered the potential for inmates to grow and harvest their own vegetables, raise and butcher their own meat, make their own clothes, and manufacture other items for use or sale by the state, such a boon to the state's budget could not reasonably be ignored.

When the doors of Auburn Prison opened in 1819, America had the model and prototype of its maximum-security prison. The New York authorities were as devoted as those in Pennsylvania to the idea of keeping prisoners isolated from each other and from the outside world. Prisoners were not even allowed to communicate with their families, except through the prison chaplain. New York's departure from the Pennsylvania system was in the commitment to provide a common work and dining area for inmates. Silence among inmates was strictly enforced, however. The New York officials were deeply committed to the view that a steady, predictable, unrelenting routine of hard work, moderate meals, silent evenings, and restful nights in individual cells would produce men who were, indeed, cured of all vices and excesses.

Because the inmates left their cells each day to work together, the cells in the Auburn-style (or congregate-style, as it came to be called) prison could be made smaller than those in the Pennsylvania-style penitentiary. The Auburn cells were primarily for sleeping and were not intended to be the prisoner's entire universe.

The inmates were awakened early and marched to work for a few hours before breakfast. After lunch they returned to their jobs until time for dinner. After the evening meal, they marched back to their individual cells to relax and sleep before going back to work the next morning. From sunrise to sunset, their days were occupied by a routine as unalterable as the solar timetable it followed.

They did not work on Sundays, and the long weekends were spent in the tiny cells that had not been designed as living quarters. On Sundays they were addressed by a prison chaplain who explained to them the wisdom and virtue of their industry and exhorted them to persevere, as all good Americans persevered, in the life of simple faith and hard work.

Penologists and reformers from throughout Europe came to America to observe the prison systems of Pennsylvania and New York. Nearly every college freshman in American reads Alexis de Tocqueville's account of "Democracy in America," but few realize that de Tocqueville was in this country, as an official emissary of the French government to study the new American prisons. France, England, Scotland, Prussia, and Germany all dispatched men to study these systems, and most European prisons since 1800 have been patterned after the solitary, Pennsylvania system. Of the two systems, de Tocqueville and his companion de Beaumont wrote, *Philadelphia system produces more honest men, and that the New York more obedient citizens.* [3]

For economic reasons, most American prisons came to be patterned after Auburn and were as much silent factories and involuntary labor pools as they were bleak prisons. Auburn Prison, in fact, turned a profit in the early years of its existence. [4]

It was an article of faith that these prisons would not only be successful in transforming idle and corrupt men into virtuous laborers, but that they were examples of model communities from which the large society could benefit as well. The Boston Prison Discipline Society reported that the Prison Program *would greatly promote order, seriousness, and purity in large families, male and female boarding schools, and colleges.* [5]

A chaplain at the Ohio Penitentiary proclaimed:

Never no never shall we see the triumph of peace, of right, of Christianity, until the daily habits of mankind shall undergo a thorough revolution. Could we all be put on prison fare, for the space of two or three generations, the world would ultimately be the better for it. Indeed, (society should) change places with the prisoners, so far as habits are concerned, taking to itself the regularity, and temperance, and sobriety of a good prison. As it is, taking this world and the next together...the prisoner has the advantage. [6]

Discipline was regarded as the key to success of the congregate prison, and one rule soon emerged as the key to discipline. That rule was silence, a silence so profound and so pervasive that it became the most awesome and striking feature of the fortress, like prisons of America. From their tour through Auburn, de Beaumont and de Tocqueville wrote:

We felt as if we traversed catacombs; there were a thousand living beings, and yet it was desert solitude. [7]

In order to maintain silence and order in the movement of large numbers of inmates about the prison, Auburn devised the silent, lock-step shuffle. Inmates stood in line, each with the right foot slightly behind the left and the right arm outstretched with the hand on the right shoulder of the man in front of him.

They moved in a shuffle, sliding the left foot forward, and then bringing the right foot to its position just behind the left, then the left again, then the right. This awkward locomotion, coupled with the striped uniforms in New York, was considered therapeutic. Prisoners were not in a state of grace with society, and their condition was made as graceless as possible, lest they forget their corrupt condition.

As the prisoners moved, they were not permitted to hold their heads up, as would befit free men, and their shameful pose with their heads turned to the right and their eyes cast to the floor kept them ever mindful of their low estate and the wickedness that had brought them there. The guard watching such a group shuffling across a prison area could readily spot any unauthorized conversation or activity.

Solitary confinement in a bare cell with one meal a day was introduced as a punishment for breaking the rules. But solitary had the disadvantage of removing prisoners from the labor force necessary to support the institution, Physical punishment, which had a less disruptive effect on inmate labor, was authorized. Soon, the very punishments that prisons were supposed to have eliminated were widely used within the prisons themselves, and the whip was the most common. Water "cures," stocks, "stretchers," and the sweatboxes were all widely used in American prisons well into the 20th century. By the 20th century, the old concept of "reformation" had largely disappeared, and most prison administrators viewed the goal of prisons as simply to keep prisoners securely in custody. Indeed, the warden's first assistant, who was responsible for the day-to-day operation of the prison, was known as the "principal keeper."

In New York State as one prison became overcrowded, another was built, always on the Auburn principle. In 1825, Sing Sing was built along the Hudson River north of New York City by a hundred inmates from Auburn who were transported down the Hudson by boat, shackled in irons. When the swelling prison population threatened the silent program and the individual cell policy, additional cell blocks were added to Auburn and Sing Sing. In 1844, the construction of Clinton Prison was authorized.

The construction of all these prisons followed the same basic plan. In fact, prison construction in the United States did not change until well into the 20th century, and even then variations were usually minor and often short-lived. From the beginning the American prison has been a maximum security institution.

As new Auburns were built throughout the country, the severity of the prison routine became the subject of criticism by a new generation of penal reformers. In 1870, the National Prison Association, at its founding meeting in Cincinnati, reminded the authorities that "reformation, not vindictive suffering should be the purpose of penal treatment of prisoners."

At the turn of the century, New York made efforts to actually implement some of the specific proposals of the Cincinnati Congress of 1870. The first such effort was Elmira Reformatory, opened in 1876 for young first **offenders**. Built on the same architectural principle as Auburn, however, it soon proved to be only another prison in the style of Auburn, but with younger inmates -- a maximum security reformatory. In 1911, Great Meadow, a new prison without a wall around it, was built for young first offenders. The striped uniforms and the silent lockstep were discontinued. The value of silence continued in actual practice in most institutions, but at Great Meadow movies were presented to the inmates once every two weeks. The dining area provided small tables with chairs in order that the young inmates could dine in a more natural atmosphere than that provided by immovable tables and stools in the other prisons.

Due to the overcrowding elsewhere, however, it was not many years before Great Meadow began receiving second offenders and other first offenders that were deemed by the authorities to require close supervision. Discipline tightened at Great Meadow; enforcement of silence appeared in the routine; and a prison factory, like those at Auburn, Sing Sing and Clinton, was started.

By 1928, a wall had been erected around the once medium security prison of the Great Meadow, and it was added to the list of adult main maximum security prisons of the state.

The architecture of prisons had become a self-engendering style. The major improvements in the construction of prisons were the introduction of escape-proof cells and unbreakable toilets and wash basins. This escalating process of constructing ever more secure prisons reached its pinnacle in 1931, when the most secure, escape-proof prison ever built opened in the little upstate village of Attica, New York. With such dedication poured into its construction, Attica was, at the time, the most expensive prison ever built. Construction had begun in 1929 and continued into the early years of the Depression. Over one hundred years had passed since inmates from Auburn had gone to work to build Sing Sing. In the spring of 1930, the scene was repeated; inmates from Auburn were transported to Attica to assist in construction.

In the late 1920s there had occurred the first "wave" or widespread outbreak of prison riots in this country. [9]

In July 1929, some 1,600 inmates of Clinton Prison rioted in protest of overcrowding there; three inmates were killed when the state put down the uprising. In the same year, Auburn Prison exploded when a trusty threw acid into a guard's face, overpowered him, and secured the keys to the prison arsenal.

Guns were passed out to several inmates and a general riot ensued in which four inmates escaped. Six shops were burned, the assistant warden was killed, and the prison was wracked before the prisoners were subdued by rifles, machine guns, and tear gas. Then, as now, New York's immediate response to the uprisings in its prisons was the appointment of official investigators and commissions to determine the causes of the sudden uprisings.

Attica State Prison in New York was to be the solution to the [then] recent problem of prison uprisings and the response to the commissions that investigated them. When Attica opened, it was widely hailed as the ultimate prison.

Its wall alone, enclosing 55 acres, was 30 feet high, extended 12 feet into the ground, and cost $1,275,000 to erect. The prison contained four separated cellblocks, each of which could house some five hundred men in individual cells. The total cost of the prison eventually reached the sum of "approximately $9,000,000."[10] The New York Times, reporting on the recent riots and the new prison under construction, stated on January 22, 1930, *whatever may be the outcome of that agitation; the immediate and practical answer to the convict revolts has been the new Attica prison.* Neither Green Haven nor any other prison since Auburn, however, has created the interest that Attica did when it was built. Shortly before it opened, Attica was hailed in the following article, which appeared in the *New York Times* on August 2, 1931:

Attica Prison to be Convict's Paradise

Condemned by the Wickersham Commission for its maintenance of Auburn and Clinton prisons, New York State will have an answer to charges of inhuman penal conditions when the New York State Prison opens at Attica within the next few months with its full quota of 2,000 convicts.

Said to be the last word in modern prison Construction, the new unit in the State's penal system will do away with such traditions as convict bunks, mess hall lockstep, bull pen's, and even locks and keys. In their places will be beds with springs and mattresses, a cafeteria with food under glass, recreation rooms and an automatic signal system by which convicts will notify guards of their presence in their cells. Doors will be operated by compressed air, sunlight will stream into cells and every prisoner will have an individual radio. [11]

Perhaps because of the depression economy, perhaps for other reasons as well, no Attica inmate has ever seen the institution described above. When Attica opened, there was no cafeteria with food under glass, no recreation room, no automatic signal system, and no sunlight streaming into the cells. There was, in fact, nothing but another huge, foreboding prison. With the unprecedented emphasis on security visible in every brick and every door, this "last word in modern prison construction," far from doing away with locks and keys made them the focal point around which all life revolved.

When Attica opened, over 130 years had passed since Auburn Prison was built; the population of New York State had changed vastly; the entire social structure of the nation had been dramatically altered; new laws and social conditions had altered the very nature of crime itself; theories of human behavior had been radically modified by the developing social sciences. In fact, everything had changed -- everything but the prisons. They were still built in the silent congregate style of Auburn.

The New York State Prison System in 1971 [11]

All persons convicted of felonies and sentenced to terms of more than one year in prison were committed to one of the facilities operated by the state's Department of Correctional Services.

Persons convicted of lesser crimes and those held under custody while awaiting trial were confined in local jails, detention houses, and penitentiaries over which the Department of Correctional Services had no jurisdiction. Persons sentenced to probation were supervised by probation officers responsible to the courts and not to the corrections department.

Because of overcrowding in its jails, the City of New York arranged with the state to board approximately three thousand city prisoners in the state prison system in 1971.

At the beginning of 1971, state correction institutions held 12,210 men and 369 women. Approximately 54.5 percent of these persons were black; 33 precepts were white; 12 percent were Spanish-speaking; and 0.5 percent was of other ethnic origin. Approximately 54 percent had been committed or convicted for violent crimes, and 56 percent of all inmates had served prison terms before. Ninety-two percent of the system's institutionalized population was housed in correctional facilities, and 8 percent were in hospitals. In addition, there were some 15,000 persons on parole.

One of the largest and costliest of such systems in the country: New York's Department of Correctional Services operated twenty-one facilities, including prisons, hospitals, reformatories, work camps, and a narcotics **rehabilitation center**. The department employed over 7,650 people and its annual budget for fiscal year 1971-72 was more than $100 million.

But the heart of the system remained the maximum security prisons where prisoners were constantly supervised, and locked in their cells at 5:00 or 6:00 pm,[12] and which provided few services other than safekeeping. At the beginning of 1971 approximately 8,250 inmates were housed in the state's six maximum, security institutions -- Auburn, Attica, Clinton, Great Meadow, Green Haven, Ossining (formerly Sing Sing). Except for Ossining, which was being converted into a testing and assignment center, these prisons were located in rural areas isolated from the cities in which the families of most of the inmates resided. Correction officers, often drawn from the surrounding communities, were almost invariably white, and unfamiliar with the life-styles of the inmates committed to their care.

The state's only minimum security facilities for males were work camps restricted to the young able-bodied. Only one narcotics **treatment center** for offenders was maintained by the state; the medium security facility at Coxsackie, in which the housing requirements, the supervision, and hours of activity were more flexible, was limited to inmates under twenty-one; and the medium security facility at Elmira was restricted to inmates under thirty. There was only one medium security institution -- at Wallkill -- for which adult males of all ages were eligible, and its capacity was limited to five hundred inmates. [13]

For 90 percent of the adult males committed to the state the only accommodations available were maximum security prisons. In these institutions, first offenders were mingled with men with long criminal careers; young men, for whom there was no place in the medium or minimum security facilities, were housed with older men; inmates who were convicted of property crimes, such as embezzlement, forgery, and cashing bad checks, were thrown in with inmates who had a history of violent crimes and sexual aberrations; and men serving short sentences were forced to accommodate themselves to a routine designed for men who would spend the rest of their lives in prison. All lived under the same conditions of constant surveillance and long hours in the cells with little to do and almost nothing to learn. All correctional personnel agreed that many inmates could be trusted with greater freedom, and would benefit from the increased programming possible at medium and minimum security institutions. But the state system was saddled with maximum security institutions like Attica, and there were no places available elsewhere. [14]

In 1965, efforts to convert the New York system from a purely custodian to a rehabilitative basis began when the Governor appointed a Special Committee to study the treatment of criminal offenders in New York State. Co-chairmen of the Special Committee were the then Commissioner of the Department of Corrections, Paul D. McGinnis, and the Chairman of the Board of Parole, Russell G. Oswald.

The Committee concluded that too little was known about the actual effects on recidivism of psychiatric and vocational programs, and that it was imperative that a system be created which would test the effect of different programs on the various types of offenders. While recommending that large-scale changes be made in the system only after "evaluation research," the Committee urged the state to abandon:

The ancient concepts of prison and reformatory, and to start working with a new concept: the correctional institution. Only then will we be able to break out of the conceptual bondage that results in what amounts to maximum security for almost all inmates of all ages. [15]

One change recommended by the Special Committee to signify this new commitment became effective on July 8, 1970. On that date the names of all the state's maximum security prisons were changed. There were no more prisons; in their places, instead, stood six maximum security "correctional facilities." The prison wardens became "institution superintendents;" and the former principal keepers became "deputy superintendents." No one's job or essential duties changed, only the title. Certainly the institutions themselves did not change. No walls crumbled, no bars disappeared, no windows opened. No attitudes were revolutionized by the euphemistic name change, and no prejudices were erased by the simple expedient of switching titles.

To a man spending fourteen to sixteen hours a day in a cell being "rehabilitated," and having little useful to do with the rest of his hours, it was scarcely any comfort and no reassurance to learn that he was suddenly "an inmate in a correctional facility," instead of a convict in prison.

Less than six months later, another broad organization change recommended by the Special Committee in 1968 restructured the entire correction system in New York. On January 1, 1971, the former Department of Correction and the Division of Parole were merged into the new Department of Correctional Services, centralizing in one agency the custody of convicted felons from the time they entered prison until they were finally released from all state supervision, including parole. However, the structural change meant nothing to the twelve thousand inmates and patients whom the new department was assigned to correct.

The Evolution of the New York Prison System [Part II]

Solitary confinement in a bare cell with one meal a day was introduced as a punishment for breaking the rules. But solitary had the disadvantage of removing prisoners from the labor force necessary to support the institution, Physical punishment, which had a less disruptive effect on inmate labor, was authorized. Soon, the very punishments that prisons were supposed to have eliminated were widely used within the prisons themselves, and the whip was the most common. Water "cures," stocks, "stretchers," and the sweatboxes were all widely used in American prisons well into the 20th century. By the 20th century, the old concept of "reformation" had largely disappeared, and most prison administrators viewed the goal of prisons as simply to keep prisoners securely in custody. Indeed, the warden's first assistant, who was responsible for the day-to-day operation of the prison, was known as the "principal keeper."

In New York, as one prison became overcrowded, another was built, always on the Auburn principle. In 1825, Sing Sing was built along the Hudson River north of New York City by a hundred inmates from Auburn who were transported down the Hudson by boat, shackled in irons. When the swelling prison population threatened the silent PROGRAM and the individual cell policy, additional cell blocks were added to Auburn and Sing Sing. In 1844, the construction of Clinton Prison was authorized.

The construction of all these prisons followed the same basic plan. In fact, prison construction in the United States did not change until well into the 20th century, and even then variations were usually minor and often short-lived. From the beginning the American prison has been a maximum **SECURITY** institution.

As new Auburns were built throughout the country, the severity of the prison routine became the subject of criticism by a new generation of penal reformers. In 1870, the National Prison Association, at its founding meeting in Cincinnati, reminded the authorities that "reformation, not vindictive suffering should be the purpose of penal treatment of prisoners."

At the turn of the century, New York made efforts to actually implement some of the specific proposals of the Cincinnati Congress of 1870. The first such effort was Elmira Reformatory, opened in 1876 for young first offenders. Built on the same architectural principle as Auburn, however, it soon proved to be only another prison in the style of Auburn, but with younger inmates -- a maximum security reformatory. In 1911, Great Meadow, a new prison without a wall around it, was built for young first offenders. The striped uniforms and the silent lockstep were discontinued. The vale of silence CONTINUED in actual practice in most institutions, but at Great Meadow movies were presented to the inmates once every two weeks. The dining area provided small tables with chairs in order that the young inmates could dine in a more natural atmosphere than that provided by immovable tables and stools in the other prisons.

Due to the overcrowding elsewhere, however, it was not many years before Great Meadow began receiving second offenders and other first offenders who were deemed by the authorities to require close supervision.

Discipline tightened at Great Meadow; enforcement of silence appeared in the routine; and a prison factory, like those at Auburn, Sing Sing and Clinton, was started. By 1928, a wall had been erected around the once medium security prison of the Great Meadow, and it was added to THE LIST of adult main maximum security prisons of the state.

The architecture of prisons had become a self-engendering style. The major improvements in the construction of prisons were the introduction of escape-proof cells and unbreakable toilets and wash basins. This escalating process of constructing ever more secure prisons reached its pinnacle in 1931, when the most secure, escape-proof prison ever built opened in the little upstate village of Attica, New York. With such dedication poured into its construction, Attica was, at the time, the most expensive prison ever built. Construction had begun in 1929 and CONTINUED into the early years of the Depression. Over one hundred years had passed since inmates from Auburn had gone to work to build Sing Sing. In the spring of 1930, the scene was repeated; inmates from Auburn were transported to Attica to assist in construction.

In the late 1920s there had occurred the first "wave" or widespread outbreak of prison riots in this country. [9] In July 1929, some 1,600 INMATES of Clinton Prison rioted in protest of overcrowding there; three inmates were killed when the state put down the uprising. In the same year, Auburn Prison exploded when a trusty threw acid into a guard's face, overpowered him, and secured the keys to the prison arsenal. Guns were passed out to several inmates and a general riot ensued in which four inmates escaped.

Six shops were burned, the assistant warden was killed, and the prison was wracked before the prisoners were subdued by rifles, machine guns, and tear gas. Then, as now, New York's immediate response to the uprisings in its prisons was the appointment of official investigators and commissions to determine the causes of the sudden uprisings.

Attica State Prison in New York was to be the solution to the [then] recent problem of prison uprisings and the response to the commissions that investigated them. When Attica OPENED, it was widely hailed as the ultimate prison. Its wall alone, enclosing 55 acres, was 30 feet high, extended 12 feet into the ground, and cost $1,275,000 to erect. The prison contained four separated cellblocks, each of which could house some five hundred men in individual cells. The total cost of the prison eventually reached the sum of "approximately $9,000,000."[10] The New York Times, reporting on the recent riots and the new prison under CONSTRUCTION, stated on January 22, 1930, *whatever may be the outcome of that agitation; the immediate and practical answer to the convict revolts has been the new Attica prison.* Neither Green Haven *nor any other prison since Auburn, however, has created the interest* that Attica did when it was built. SHORTLY before it opened, Attica was hailed in the following article, which appeared in the *New York Times* on August 2, 1931:

ATTICA PRISON TO BE CONVICT'S PARADISE

Condemned by the Wickersham Commission for its MAINTENANCE of Auburn and Clinton prisons, New York State will have an answer to charges of inhuman penal conditions when the New York State Prison opens at Attica within the next few months with its full quota of 2,000 convicts. aid to be the last word in modern prison construction, the new unit in the State's penal system will do away with such traditions as convict bunks, mess hall lockstep, bull pens, and even locks and keys. In their places will be beds with springs and mattresses, a cafeteria with food under glass, recreation rooms and an automatic signal system by which convicts will notify guards of their presence in their cells. Doors will be operated by compressed air, sunlight will stream into cells and every prisoner will have an individual radio. [11]

Perhaps because of the Depression economy, perhaps for other reasons as well, no Attica INMAET has ever seen the institution described above. When Attica OPENED, there was no cafeteria with food under glass, no recreation room, no automatic signal system, and no sunlight streaming into the cells. There was, in fact, nothing but another huge, foreboding prison. With the unprecedented emphasis on security visible in every brick and every door, this "last word in modern prison construction," far from doing away with locks and keys made them the focal point around which all life revolved.

When Attica opened, over 130 years had passed since Auburn Prison was built; the population of New York State had changed vastly; the entire social structure of the nation had been dramatically altered; new laws and social conditions had altered the very nature of crime itself; theories of human behavior had been radically modified by the developing social sciences. In fact, everything had changed -- everything but the prisons. They were still built in the silent congregate style of Auburn.

The Evolution of the New York Prison System [Part III]

THE NEW YORK STATE PRISON SYSTEM IN 1971 [11]

All persons convicted of felonies and sentenced to terms of more than one year in prison were committed to one of the facilities operated by the state's Department of Correctional Services. Persons convicted of lesser crimes and those held under custody while awaiting trial were confined in local jails, detention houses, and penitentiaries over which the Department of Correctional Services had no jurisdiction. Persons sentenced to probation were supervised by probation officers responsible to the courts and not to the CORRECTIONS department. Because of overcrowding in its jails, the City of New York ARRANGED with the state to board approximately three thousand city prisoners in the state prison system in 1971.

At the BEGINNING of 1971, state correction institutions held 12,210 men and 369 women. Approximately 54.5 percent of these persons were black; 33 percent were white; 12 percent were Spanish-speaking; and 0.5 percent were of other ethnic origin. Approximately 54 percent had been committed or convicted for violent crimes, and 56 percent of all INMATES had served prison terms before. Ninety-two percent of the system's institutionalized population were housed in correctional facilities, and 8 percent were in hospitals. In addition, there were some 15,000 persons on parole.

One of the largest and costliest of such systems in the country: New York's Department of Correctional Services operated twenty-one facilities, including prisons, hospitals, reformatories, work camps, and a narcotics rehabilitation center. The department EMPLOYED over 7,650 people and its annual budget for fiscal year 1971-72 was more than $100 million.

But the heart of the system remained the maximum SECURITY prisons where prisoners were constantly supervised, and locked in their cells at 5:00 or 6:00 pm, [12] and which provided few services other than safekeeping. At the beginning of 1971 approximately 8,250 INMATES were housed in the state's six maximum, security institutions -- Auburn, Attica, Clinton, Great Meadow, Green Haven, Ossining (formerly Sing Sing). Except for Ossining, which was being converted into a testing and assignment center, these prisons were located in rural areas isolated from the cities in which the families of most of the inmates resided. Correction officers, often drawn from the surrounding communities, were almost invariably white, and unfamiliar with the life-styles of the inmates committed to their care.

The state's only minimum security facilities for males were work camps restricted to the young able-bodied. Only one narcotics treatment center for offenders was maintained by the state; the medium security facility at Coxsackie, in which the housing requirements, the supervision, and hours of activity were more flexible, was limited to inmates under twenty-one; and the medium security facility at Elmira was restricted to inmates under thirty.

There was only one medium security institution -- at Wallkill -- for which adult males of all ages were eligible, and its capacity was limited to five hundred inmates. [13]

For 90 percent of the adult males committed to the state the only accommodations available were maximum security prisons. In these institutions, first offenders were mingled 'with men with long criminal careers; young men, for whom there was no place in the medium or minimum security facilities, were housed with older men; inmates who were convicted of property crimes, such as embezzlement, forgery, and cashing bad CHECKS, were thrown in with inmates who had a history of violent crimes and sexual aberrations; and men serving short sentences were forced to accommodate themselves to a routine designed for men who would spend the rest of their lives in prison. All lived under the same conditions of constant surveillance and long hours in the cells with little to do and almost nothing to learn. All correctional personnel agreed that many inmates could be trusted with greater freedom, and would benefit from the increased programming possible at medium and minimum security institutions. But the state system was saddled with maximum security institutions like Attica, and there were no places available elsewhere. [14]

In 1965, efforts to convert the New York system from a purely custodian to a rehabilitative basis began when the Governor appointed a Special Committee to study the treatment of criminal offenders in New York State. Co-chairmen of the Special Committee were the then Commissioner of the Department of Corrections, Paul D. McGinnis, and the Chairman of the Board of Parole, Russell G. Oswald.

The Committee concluded that too little was known about the actual effects on recidivism of psychiatric and vocational PROGRAMS, and that it was imperative that a system be created which would test the effect of different programs on the various types of offenders. While recommending that large-scale changes be made in the system only after "evaluation research," the Committee urged the state to abandon:

the ancient concepts of prison and reformatory, and to start working with a now concept: the correctional institution. Only then will we be able to break out of the conceptual bondage that results in what amounts to maximum SECURITY for almost all inmates of all ages.[15]

One change recommended by the Special Committee to signify this new commitment became effective on July 8, 1970. On that date the names of all the state's maximum SECURITY prisons were changed. There were no more prisons; in their places, instead, stood six maximum security "correctional facilities." The prison wardens became "institution superintendents;" and the former principal keepers became "deputy superintendents." No one's job or essential duties changed, only the title. Certainly the institutions themselves did not change. No walls crumbled, no bars disappeared, no windows opened. No attitudes were revolutionized by the euphemistic name change, and no prejudices were erased by the simple expedient of switching titles.

To a man spending fourteen to sixteen hours a day in a cell being "rehabilitated," and having little useful to do with the rest of his hours, it was scarcely any comfort and no reassurance to learn that he was suddenly" an INMATE in a correctional facility," instead of a convict in prison.

Less than six months later, another broad organization change recommended by the Special Committee in 1968 restructured the entire CORRECTION system in New York. On January 1, 1971, the former Department of Correction and the Division of Parole were merged into the new Department of Correctional Services, centralizing in one agency the custody of convicted felons from the time they ENTERED prison until they were finally released from all state supervision, including parole. However, the structural change meant nothing to the twelve thousand inmates and patients whom the new department was assigned to correct.

Chapter 12

Corrections

"Private vs. Public Facilities, Is it cost effective and safe?"
Adrian Smith, June 11, 2012

A private prison, jail, or detention center is a place in which individuals are physically confined or interned by a third party that is contracted by a local, state or federal government agency. Private prison companies typically enter into contractual agreements with local, state, or federal governments that commit prisoners and then pay a per diem or monthly rate for each prisoner confined in the facility. Today, the privatization of prisons refers both to the takeover of existing public facilities by private operators and to the building and operation of new and additional prisons by for-profit prison companies.

The privatization movement can be traced to the contracting out of confinement and care of prisoners after the American Revolution. Deprived of the ability to ship criminals and undesirables to the Colonies, Great Britain began placing them on hulks moored in English ports (Campbell, 2001). The partial transfer of San Quentin prison administration from private to public did not mark the end of privatization. The next phase began with the Reconstruction Period (1865–1876) in the south, after the end of the Civil War. Farmers and businessmen needed to find replacements for the labor force once their slaves had been freed. Beginning in 1868, convict leases were issued to private parties to supplement their workforce (Todd, 2005). This system remained in place until the early 20th century.

Federal and state government has a long history of contracting out specific services to private firms, including medical services, food preparation, vocational training, and inmate transportation. The 1980s, though, ushered in a new era of prison privatization. With a burgeoning prison population resulting from the War on Drugs and increased use of incarceration, prison overcrowding and rising costs became increasingly problematic for local, state, and federal governments.

In response to this expanding **criminal justice** system, private business interests saw an opportunity for expansion, and consequently, private-sector involvement in prisons moved from the simple contracting of services to contracting for the **complete** management and operation of entire prisons ("Sentencing Project", 2004).

The modern private prison business first emerged and established itself publicly in 1984 when the Corrections Corporation of America (CCA) was awarded a contract to take over a facility in Hamilton County, Tennessee. This marked the first time that any government in the country had contracted out the complete operation of a jail to a private operator (Jail Breaks, 2001). The following year, CCA gained further public attention when it offered to take over the entire state prison system of Tennessee for $200 million. The bid was ultimately defeated due to strong opposition from public employees and the skepticism of the state legislature (Bates, 1998). Despite that initial defeat, CCA since then has successfully expanded, as have other for-profit prison companies. As of December 2000, there were 153 private correctional facilities (prisons, jails and detention centers) operating in the United States with a capacity of over 119,000.

Private companies in the United States operate *264 correctional facilities, housing almost 99,000 adult offenders* (Schmalleger, F., & Smykla, J. (2007, 2005, 2002) Companies operating such facilities include the Corrections Corporation of America, the GEO Group, In, and Community Education Centers. The GEO Group was formerly known as Wackenhut Securities, and includes the Cornell Companies, which merged with GEO in 2010.

Corrections Corporation of America (CCA) has a capacity of more than 80,000 beds in 65 correctional facilities. The GEO Group operates 61 facilities with a capacity of 49,000 offender beds.

Most privately run facilities are located in the southern and western portions of the United States and include both state and federal offenders. Proponents of privately run prisons contend that cost-savings and efficiency of operation place private prisons at an advantage over public prisons and support the argument for privatization, but some research casts doubt on the validity of these arguments, as evidence has shown that private prisons are neither demonstrably more cost-effective, nor more efficient than public prisons. An evaluation of 24 different studies on cost-effectiveness revealed that, at best, results of the question are inconclusive and, at worst, there is no difference in cost-effectiveness.

A study by the U.S. Bureau of Justice Statistics found that the cost-savings promised by private prisons "have simply not materialized." Some research has concluded that for-profit prisons cost more than public prisons. Furthermore, cost estimates from privatization advocates may be misleading, because private facilities often refuse to accept inmates that cost the most to house. A 2001 study concluded that a pattern of sending less expensive inmates to privately-run facilities artificially inflated cost savings. A 2005 study found that Arizona's public facilities were seven times more likely to house violent offenders and three times more likely to house those convicted of more serious offenses.

Evidence suggests that lower staff levels and training at private facilities may lead to increases in incidences of violence and escapes. A nationwide study found that assaults on guards by inmates were 49 percent more frequent in private prisons than in government-run prisons. The same study revealed that assaults on fellow inmates were 65 percent more frequent in private prison (Austin, Conventry, 2001).

After a complete analysis on private vs. public run correctional facilities, one may come to the conclusion that private run facilities are no more cost saving effective or safer than a state run facility. We must ask ourselves, is any monetary amount worth the lives of one of our own? The statistics are there, this profession is tough enough, we should take pride of it and not risk the lives of our bravest officers just to attempt to save the state a couple of dollars.

Chapter 13

The Economic Collapse

"Private Prisons: The More Americans They Put Behind Bars the More Money They Make"
Michael Snyder, March 11th, 2013 [2]

How would you describe an industry that wants to put more Americans in prison and keep them there longer so that it can **make more money**? In America today, approximately 130,000 people are locked up in private prisons that are being run by for-profit companies, and that number is growing very rapidly. Overall, the U.S. has approximately 25 percent of the entire global prison population even though it only has 5 percent of the total global population. The United States has the highest incarceration rate on the entire globe by far, and no nation in the history of the world has ever locked up more of its own citizens than we have. Are we really such a cesspool of filth and decay that we need to lock up so many of our own people? Or are there some other factors at work? Could part of the problem be that we have allowed companies to lock up men and women in cages for profit? The two largest private prison companies combined to bring in close to $3,000,000,000 in revenue in 2010, and the largest private prison companies have spent tens of millions of dollars on lobbying and campaign contributions over the past decade. Putting Americans behind bars has become very big business, and those companies have been given a perverse incentive to push for even more Americans to be locked up. It is a system that is absolutely teeming with corruption, and it is going to get a lot worse unless someone does something about it.

One of the keys to success in the private prison business it to get politicians to vote your way. That is why the big private prison companies spend so much money on lobbying and campaign contributions.

The following is an excerpt from a report put out by the Justice **Policy** Institute entitled "Gaming the System: How the Political Strategies of Private Prison Companies Promote Ineffective Incarceration Policies"

For-profit private prison companies primary use three strategies to influence policy: lobbying, direct campaign contributions, and building relationships, networks, and associations.

Over the years, these political strategies have allowed private prison companies to promote policies that lead to higher rates of incarceration and thus greater profit margins for their company. In particular, private prison companies have had either influence over or helped to draft model legislation such as "three-strikes" and "truth-in-sentencing" laws, both of which have driven up incarceration rates and ultimately created more opportunities for private prison companies to bid on contracts to increase revenues.

If you can believe it, three of the largest private prison companies have spent approximately $45,000,000 combined on lobbying and campaign contributions over the past decade.

Would they be spending so much money if those companies did not believe that it was getting results?

Just look at what has happened to the U.S. prison population over the past several decades. Prior to 1980, there were virtually no private prisons in the United States. But since that time, we have seen the overall prison population and the private prison population absolutely explode.

For example, between 1990 and 2009 the number of Americans in private prisons grew by about 1600 percent.

Overall, the U.S. prison population more than quadrupled between 1980 and 2007. So something has definitely changed.

Not that it is wrong to put people in prison when they commit crimes. Of course not and right now violent crime is rapidly rising in many of our largest cities. When people commit violent crimes they need to be removed from the streets.

But when you put those criminals into the hands of private companies that are just in it to make a buck, the potential for abuse is enormous.

For example, when auditors visited one private prison in Texas, they "got so much faecal matter on their shoes they had to wipe their feet on the grass outside."

The prisoners were literally living in their own manure.

How would you feel if a member of your own family was locked up in such a facility?

And the truth is that there seem to be endless stories of abuse in private prisons. One private prison company reportedly charges inmates $5.00 a minute to make phone calls but only pays them $1.00 a day to work.

Last year the Corrections Corporation of America (CCA), the nation's largest private prison company, received $74 million of taxpayers' money to run immigration detention centers. Their largest facility in Lumpkin, Georgia, receives $200 a night for each of the 2,000 detainees it holds, and rakes in yearly profits between $35 million and $50 million.

Prisoners held in this remote facility depend on the prison's phones to communicate with their lawyers and loved ones. Exploiting inmates' need, CCA charges detainees here $5 per minute to make phone calls. Yet the prison only pays inmates who work at the facility $1 a day. At that rate, it would take five days to pay for just one minute.

Speaking of work, private prisons have found that exploiting their inmates as a source of slave labor can be extraordinarily profitable. Today, private prisons are stealing jobs from ordinary American workers in a whole host of industries. The following is from an article by Vicky Pelaez.

According to the Left Business Observer, the federal prison industry produces 100% of all military helmets, ammunition belts, bullet-proof vests, ID tags, shirts, pants, tents, bags and canteens. Along with war supplies, prison workers supply 985 of the entire market for equipment assembly services; 93% of paints and paintbrushes; 92% of stove assembly; 46% of body armor; 36% of home appliances, 30% of headphones / microphones / speakers; and 21% of office furniture. Airplane parts, medical supplies, and much more: prisoners are even raising seeing-eye dogs for blind people.

And many of the largest corporations in America have rushed in to take advantage of this pool of very cheap slave labor. Just check out some of the big names that have been exploiting prison labor.

At least 37 states have legalized the contracting of prison labor by private corporations that mount their operations inside state prisons. The list of such companies contains the cream of U.S. Corporate society. IBM, Boeing, Motorola, Microsoft, AT&T, Wireless, Texas Instrument, Dell, Compaq, Honeywell, Hewlett-Packard, Nortel, Lucent Technologies, 3Com, Intel, Northern Telecom, TWA, Nordsrom's, Revlon, Macy's, Pierre Cardin, Target Stores, and many more. All of these businesses are excited about the economic boom generation by prison labor. Just between 1980 and 1994, profits went up from $392 million to $1.31 billion.

Inmates in state penitentiaries generally receive the minimum wage for their work, but not all, in Colorado, the get about $2 per hour, well under the minimum. And in privately-run prisons, they receive as 17 cents per hour for a maximum of six hours a day, the equivalent of $20 per month. The highest-paying private prison is CCA in Tennessee, where prisoners receive 50 cents per hour for what they call "highly skilled positions." At those rates, it is no surprise that inmates find the pay in federal prisons to be very generous. There, they can earn $1.25 an hour and work eights a day and sometimes overtime. They can send home $200-$300 per month.

But of course some of the biggest profits for private prisons come from detaining young people. Today, private prison companies operate more than 50 percent of all "youth correctional facilities" in the United States.

And sometimes judges have even been bribed by these companies to sentence kids to very harsh sentences and to send them to their facilities. The following is from a report about two judges in Pennsylvania that were recently convicted for taking money to send kids to private prisons...

US Attorney Bill Houser talks with the media after the sentencing of Michael Conahan Friday in Federal Court Scranton. Clark Van Orden US Attorney Bill Houser talks with the media after the sentencing of Michael Conahan Friday in Federal Court Scranton. February 19. 2013 4:40AM

Conahan sentenced to 17.5 years [1]

Michael Conahan, a former jurist in Luzerne County, was sentenced on Friday to 210 months in custody by Senior U.S. District Court Judge Edwin M. Kosik II. Conahan was also ordered to pay $874,000 in restitution. As Main Justice reported in August, Ciavarella, former president judge of the Court of Common Pleas and former judge of the Juvenile Court for Luzerne County, was sentenced to 28 years in prison and ordered to make restitution of $965,930.

Conahan's role in the "cash for kids" scheme was to order the closing of a county-run detention center, clearing the way for Ciavarella, once known as a strict "law and order" judge, to send young offenders to private facilities. This arrangement worked out well for Ciavarella and Conahan, as well as the builder of the facilities and a developer, who pleaded guilty to lesser charges.

The arrangement didn't work out so well for the young offenders, some of them sent away for offenses that were little more than pranks and would have merited probation, or perhaps just scolding's, if the judges had tried to live up to their oaths.

Chapter 14

"The Sentencing Project"

Since the early 1970s the prison and jail population in the United States has increased at an unprecedented rate. The more than 500% rise in the number of people incarcerated in the nation's prisons and jails has resulted in a total of 2.2 million people behind bars.

This growth has been accompanied by an increasingly disproportionate racial composition, with particularly high rates of incarceration for African Americans, who now constitute 900,000 of the total 2.2 million incarcerated populations. The exponential increase in the use of incarceration has had modest success at best in producing public safety,[1] while contributing to family disruption and the weakening of informal social controls in many African American communities. Overall, data from the Bureau of Justice Statistics document that one in six black men had been incarcerated as of 2001. If current trends continue, one in three black males born today can expect to spend time in prison during his lifetime.[2] The prevalence of imprisonment for women is considerably lower than for men, but many of the same racial disparities persist, with black women being more likely to be incarcerated than white women.[3]

While the disproportionate rate of incarceration for African Americans has been well documented for some time, a significant development in the past decade has been the growing proportion of the Hispanic population entering prisons and jails.[4]

In 2005, Hispanics comprised 20% of the state and federal prison population, a rise of 43% since 1990.[5] As a result of these trends, one of every six Hispanic males and one of every 45 Hispanic females born today can expect to go to prison in his or her lifetime.[6] These rates are more than double those for non-Hispanic whites.

While these national figures are disturbing, they mask the extreme state-level variations in the impact of incarceration on communities of color. This report examines racial and ethnic dynamics of incarceration by state and highlights new information that extends the findings of previous analyses[7] by including data on jail populations and the impact of incarceration on the Hispanic community.[8]

Highlights of this analysis include:

1. African Americans are incarcerated at nearly six (5.6) times the rate of whites;

2. Hispanics are incarcerated at nearly double (1.8) the rate of whites;

3. States exhibit substantial variation in the ratio of black-to-white incarceration, ranging from a high of 13.6-to-1 in Iowa to a low of 1.9-to-1 in Hawaii;

4. States with the highest black-to-white ratio are disproportionately located in the Northeast and Midwest, including the leading states of Iowa, Vermont, New Jersey, Connecticut, and Wisconsin. This geographic concentration is true as well for the Hispanic-to-white ratio, with the most disproportionate states being Massachusetts, Pennsylvania, New York, New Hampshire, and New Jersey; and,

5. States exhibiting high Black or Hispanic ratios of incarceration compared to whites fall into two categories: 1) those such as Wisconsin and Vermont which have high rates of black incarceration and average rates of white incarceration; and, 2) states such as New Jersey and Connecticut which have average rates of black incarceration and below-average rates of white incarceration. In both cases, the ratio of incarceration by race is higher than average.

National Picture: Substantial Racial Disparity

The American prison and jail system is defined by an entrenched racial disparity in the population of incarcerated people. The national incarceration rate for whites is 412 per 100,000 residents, compared to 2,290 for African Americans, and 742 for Hispanics.[9] These figures mean that 2.3% of all African Americans are incarcerated, compared to 0.4% of whites and 0.7% of Hispanics.

Racial and Ethnic Rates of Incarceration

Racial / Ethnic Group Rate Per 100,000

White	412
Black	2,290
Hispanic	742

While these overall rates of incarceration are all at record highs, they fail to reflect the concentrated impact of incarceration among young African American males in particular, many of whom reside in disadvantaged neighborhoods. One in nine (11.7%) African-American males between the ages of 25 and 29 is currently incarcerated in a prison or jail.[10]

Moreover, the uneven geographic distribution of incarceration in communities of color means that the effects of this situation radiate beyond the individual to the broader community. For example, criminologists James Lynch and William Sabol found that three percent of a single Ohio county's census block groups[11] comprised 20% of the state prison population.[12] This concentration among young males presents profound long-term consequences for employment prospects, family formation, and general quality of life.

U.S. State and Federal Prison Population, 1925-2013

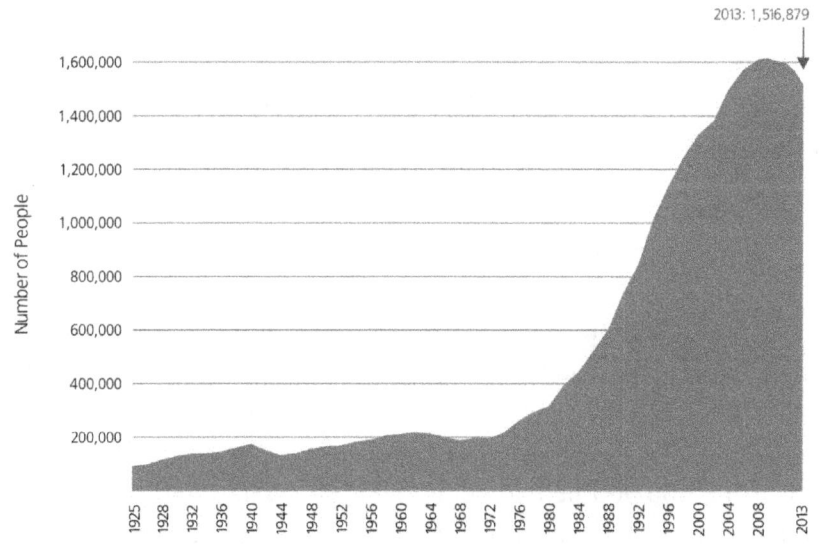

Chapter 15

"The-Greed-of-Private-Prisons"

Brian Magee (originally published at *Humanist Network News,*
August 2013

A small but increasing amount of attention over the past decade is being paid to the increased use of private prisons in the U.S. Statistics are now showing that locking people up for the profit is overriding the concept of jailing people in the name of justice.

A recent Associated Press investigation has determined one of the causes for a sharp increase in private prisons is the rise in the number of people locked up on immigration charges. In reaction to the 9/11 attacks, the country made changes to immigration laws that made it easier to detain more people and ended up being a major source of increased revenue for the country's private prison companies. The federal government uses contractors to keep nearly half of the 400,000 people being held on immigration charges. The AP also reports that "nearly every aspect" of a huge budget increase to house those charged with immigration violations in 2005 was given to private prison companies.

There exists a "mutually beneficial and evidently legal relationship between those who make corrections and immigration policy and a few prison companies," the report concluded, adding that there's essentially no cost savings being achieved, the main selling point used by those advocating for private prisons. The cost to house a prisoner being held by U.S. Immigrations and Customs Enforcement has risen from $80 per person, per day in 2004 to $166 today, with the government refusing to provide details explaining the difference.

According to the AP report, "A decade ago, more than 3,300 criminal immigrants were sent to private prisons under two 10-year contracts the Federal Bureau of Prisons signed with [Corrections Corporation of America] worth $760 million. Now, the agency is paying the private companies $5.1 billion to hold more than 23,000 criminal immigrants through 13 contracts of varying lengths."

Three companies receive the bulk of the prison contracts in the U.S.: Corrections Corporation of America (CCA), The GEO Group, and Management and Training Corp. Private Prison companies now house about half of the country's prisons, up from only about 10% a decade ago.

The money these companies have spent on lobbying and a campaign donation is estimated to be at least $45 million over the last decade, the AP found. The result has been hundreds of millions of dollars in yearly profits.

Despite industry assurances to the contrary, a report from the Justice Policy Institute (JPI) last year indicated that lobbying efforts and campaign donations by private prison companies and their employees are done in are done in order "to make money through harsh policies and longer sentences." Similar to the conclusion of the AP investigation about the relationship between lawmakers and private prison companies, the JPI report concludes "the relationship between government officials and private prison companies has been part of the fabric of the industry from the start."

A primary fear of this kind of relationship–a direct connection between those with power to send people to prison and the prisons themselves–has already happened. In Pennsylvania a judge has been given 17 years in prison for sentencing juveniles to a private facility in a "cash for kids" scandal. Many of those sent to private facilities were locked up from minor offences not normally subject to incarceration.

In another instance of abuse, it was reported that CCA was charging inmates five dollars per minute for phone calls at one facility in Georgia.

It's not only immigration and juvenile detention scams that are allowing private prison companies to millions of dollars in yearly profits. Drug users are another huge source of people to fill the growing number of private prison cells.

In a 2008 *New York Times* story titled "U.S. prison population dwarfs that of other nations," it was pointed out that there were about 40,000 people in jails for drug offenses in 1980, much less than the 50,000 that were currently in jail on drug charges at the time. According to The Sentencing Project, those federal prisons on drug charges have risen from 4,749 in 1980 to 97,472 in 2010. Over half of all people in federal prisons are there for drug crimes.

The *Times* story puts the number of prisoners at 2.3 million and points out it is even more that the 1.6 million people China has in prisons, despite the fact that they have a population four times as large as the U.S. The reasons given by the *Times* for the huge numbers of people in U.S. jails and prisons are varied, but they include "higher levels of violent crime, harsher sentencing laws, a legacy of racial turmoil, a special fervor in combating illegal drugs, the American temperament, and the lack of a social safety net. Even democracy plays a role, as judges – many of whom are elected, another American anomaly – yield to populist demands for tough justice."

Stevenson adds that the increases also come from our response to poverty, mental illness, and race, among other factors, including "misguided three strikes laws" and harsh penalties for minors – things hardly any other country does. The *Times* story points out that Canada's incarceration rate has remained stable while its crime rate has closely paralleled the U.S. For example, the average prison term for a burglar in the U.S. is 16 months while in Canada it's only five months.

In addition to investors in private prisons pushing for their increased use to increase revenues, prison guard unions are lobbying to stop reforms that would allow for more early release eligibility and shorter sentences. If there are fewer prisoners, there is a reduced need for guards which reduces the size and strength of the unions, providing a motivation to work against any move that would reduce the number of those behind bars.

There are efforts to challenging the move toward private prisons and maintaining long prison sentences for more people. The National Prison Divestment Campaign, launched in 2011, is one example. It is a coalition of groups pushing to get investors to pull out of private prison companies. The campaign is made up of religious groups, immigrant rights organizations and others with a criminal justice focus. The campaign has seen some successes in getting financial managers to pull funds from the private prison companies, as well as getting other companies, such as food suppliers, from not doing businesses with them.

A profit motive is always going to influence public policy, which means justice and simple fairness can easily be overrun by those looking to make money, especially when lawmakers are looking out for a company's profits, not its country's citizen. With our country being a world leader when it comes to the numbers of people we put in prisons and jails, it's an obvious target for those looking to make money, the same as it would be for any growth industry. Because businesses are in place to make money for its owners, any conflict with other factors–like justice and fairness–are secondary at best.

If we want to save money in the prison system while working to advance system of reasonable justice, the answer is not to privatize our prisons–adding the additional costs of maintaining large profits and funding lobbying costs–but to reduce the number of prisoners and the sentences they serve. It is immoral to create a system that has within it the motivation of money when it comes to takes away anyone's freedom. No matter how many safeguards are promised, the greed brought to life by guaranteed profits paid for taxpayers will always win. The only solution is to remove greed as much as possible from the structure.

Chapter 16

"NYS Department of Corrections and Community Supervision"

Purpose of the Report

This report presents information on inmates and incarcerated parolees held under Department of Corrections and Community Supervision (DOCCS) custody as of January 1, 2014. It profiles under custody offenders' demographic and criminal history characteristics.

Additional Offenders Reported Due to the Merger of Corrections and Parole

On April 1, 2011, the former Division of Parole and the former Department of Correctional Services merged to form the Department of Corrections and Community Supervision (DOCCS). In past years the Department's Under Custody reports only included inmates in correctional facilities. Starting with the 2012 report, all inmates are reported including those participating in the Alt 90 or Alt 45 programs. In addition, "incarcerated parolees" (offenders under community supervision who are participating in a parole program at a DOCCS facility) will be included, but reported separately. Most "incarcerated parolees" are housed in parole program facilities, while some are housed in correctional facilities. Similarly, most inmates are housed in correctional facilities, while a few others are housed in parole program facilities.

The table below shows the distribution of the various offender subgroups within the under custody population.

Descriptions of these different offender subgroups are presented on the next page.

Profile of Inmate Population
Under Custody on January 1, 2014

Executive Summary

Characteristics	Category	Inmates Under Custody	Incarcerated Parolees Under Custody	Total Under Custody
Population Jan 1, 2014		53,565	577	54,142
Gender	Male	95.5%	90.3%	95.5%
	Female	4.4%	9.7%	4.5%
	Average Age	37.8	32.0	37.8
Race / Ethnic Status	White	23.8%	45.6%	24.1%
	African-American	49.3%	37.8%	49.2%
	Hispanic	24.1%	14.2%	24.0%
Region	New York City	45.8%	18.7%	45.5%
	Suburban New York	11.1%	7.8%	11.1%
	Upstate	43.1%	73.5%	43.4%
World Region of Birth	Foreign Born	9.8%	3.3%	9.7%
Marital Status	Never Married	65.7%	79.9%	65.9%
Living Children	One or more living children	59.3%	59.3&	59.4%
Religious Affiliation	Catholic	23.5%	27.9%	23.5%
	Protestant	27.1%	23.6%	27.0%
	Islam	11.4%	6.4%	11.4%
Military Service Veteran Status	Veteran	3.8%	1.4%	4.0%
Minimum Sentence	Median Minimum (in months)	64.0	24.0	62.0

	Average Minimum (in months)	122.0	28.2	121.0
Maximum Sentence	Median time in months	84.0	42.0	84.0
	Average Minimum (in months)	140.5	47.8	139.5
Crime	Violent Felony	65.5%	8.5%	64.9%
	Drug Offenses	12.0%	41.2%	12.3%
	Property / Other	12.7%	39.7%	12.9%
Second Felony Offender Status	First Felony	56.4%	49.7%	56.3%
	Second Felony	39.3%	50.1%	39.5%
	Persistent Felony	4.3%	0.2%	4.3%
Prior Adult Criminal Record	No Prior Arrest	16.2%	6.9%	16.1%
	Prior Prison Term	33.5%	22.0%	33.4%
Time Served in Department Custody	Median time served (in months)	24.8	1.4	N/A
	Average time (in months)	60.3	1.8	N/A
Time to Earliest Release Date	Median time (in months)	15.9	*	*
	Average time (in months)	50.7	*	*
Determinate Sentence	Drug Offenses - Determinate	*	*	93.9%
	Violent Felony - Determinate	*	*	68.7%
Education	Verified High School Diploma	59.1%	58.4%	59.0
OMH Mental Health Service Level	OMH Level 1 - 4	16.1%	19.1%	16.1%
* Not reported				

http://www.doccs.ny.gov/Research/Reports/2014/UnderCustody_Report_2014.pdf

Types of Facility Inmates	Inmates	Incarcerated Parolees	Total
Correctional Facilities	53,221	133	53,354
Parole Program Facilities	344	444	788
Total	53,565	577	54,142

1. Alt-90 cases have been assigned to an alternative 90-day drug treatment program at Willard Drug Treatment Campus (DTC), while Alt-45 cases have been assigned to an alternative 45-day drug treatment program at Edgecombe Residential Treatment Facility.

Offender Categories

Inmates in correctional facilities are inmates who have been sentenced to prison (or returned to prison as a result of a parole violation), are not under community supervision, and are incarcerated in a traditional "prison" facility (N=53,221).

Inmates in parole program facilities are returned parole violators who are participating in an alternative drug treatment program. These inmates were revoked and given a time assessment by an Administrative Law Judge (ALJ) that represents a period of time that they must spend in prison. However, in lieu of serving the full amount of time in prison, these offenders were offered the opportunity to participate in a drug treatment program and they have volunteered to do so. If they successfully complete the program (either 90 days at Willard Drug Treatment Campus or 45 days at Edgecombe Residential Treatment Facility), these offenders will be released from incarceration at the completion of the program and restored to community supervision. If they do not successfully complete the drug treatment program, they must complete the remainder of their time assessment in a correctional facility (N=344).

Incarcerated parolees in correctional facilities are parolees who are under community supervision and have been incarcerated in order to participate in a treatment program at a parole program facility (e.g. Willard Drug Treatment Campus, Edgecombe Residential Treatment Facility).

Incarcerated parolees in correctional facilities (N=133) are in one of the following situations: 1) in a reception facility on the way to beginning a treatment program in a parole program facility, 2) in a correctional facility awaiting an outcome hearing by an administrative law judge as a result of being removed from a treatment program at a parole program facility, or 3) are participating in an alternative treatment program due to medical or mental health needs that cannot be met at the designated parole program facility.

Incarcerated parolees in parole program facilities are parolees who are under community supervision and participating in an assigned treatment program at a parole program facility. Once these incarcerated parolees complete the treatment program, they will be returned to the community to complete their term of community supervision. If these incarcerated parolees do not successfully complete their assigned treatment program, they will be removed from the program and the parole violation process will proceed accordingly. Parolees who fail the Willard Drug Treatment program and parolees who were sent to Edgecombe via special condition are removed from the programs and a violation warrant is issued. Parolees who were sent to Edgecombe with the issuance of a warrant are removed from the program and a final hearing is scheduled (N=444).

Sections of the Report

The first section of this report describes the demographic characteristics of inmates and incarcerated parolees, including gender, age, race/ethnicity, and region of commitment, birthplace, and marital status, number of living children, religious affiliation, and veteran status.

The second section describes the criminal history of inmates and incarcerated parolees, including information on minimum sentence, commitment crime, second felony sentencing status, prior adult criminal record, length of time served at current facility, length of time in Department custody, time to earliest release, and determinant sentencing status.

Gender Distribution

There were 54,142 offenders under custody on January 1, 2014. Of this total, 51,729 (96%) were male and 2,413 (4%) were female. There was a drop of 723 (-1%) total offenders under custody since last year. The number of male offenders decreased by 835 (-2%) while female offenders increased by 112 (5%). Females made up a larger proportion of incarcerated parolees (10%) than inmates (4%).

Race / Ethnic Status by Gender (2014)

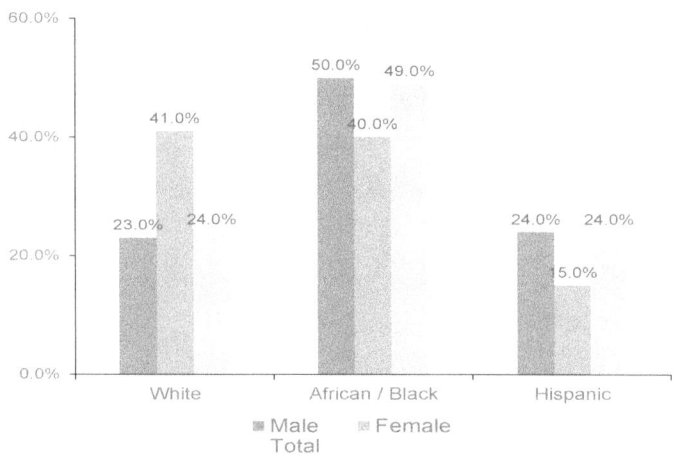

Region of Commitment

Approximately half (46%) of the offenders under custody on January 1, 2014 were committed from New York City and 11% were committed from suburban New York (Nassau, Rockland, Suffolk, and Westchester counties). Upstate counties with a population center of 50,000 inhabitants or more (Albany, Broome, Erie, Monroe, Oneida, Onondaga, Niagara, Rensselaer, and Schenectady counties) comprised 25% of the under custody population. The remaining 19% were sentenced from the other Upstate counties. The incarcerated parolee population was less likely than inmates to have been committed from New York City (19% vs. 46%) and more likely to have been committed from Upstate other counties (42% vs. 19%).

When compared with males under custody, females under custody were less likely to come from New York City (34% vs. 46%) and were more likely to come from Upstate other (30% vs. 18%).

Region of Commitment by Gender (2014)

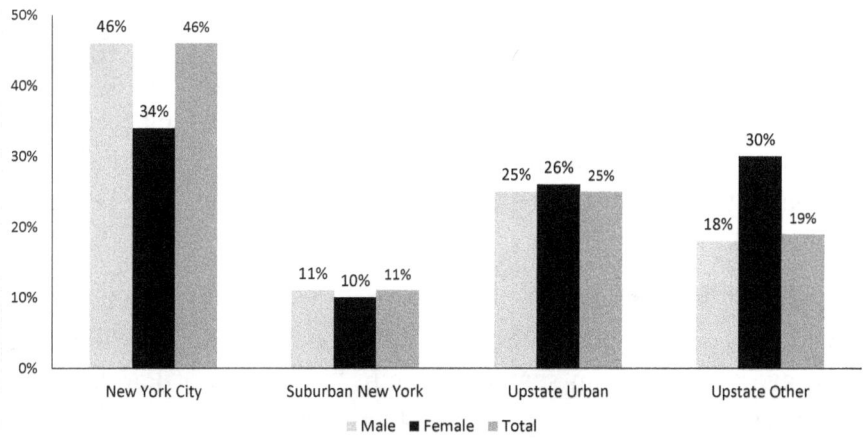

Time to Earliest Release

Time to earliest release date is a measure of the length of time until the earliest possible date at which the inmate can legally be released. Incarcerated parolees are not included in this section.

Sixty percent (60%) of the inmate population had less than two years to their earliest release dates. The average time to earliest release for the under custody population on January 1, 2013, was 51 months. The median time to earliest release was 16 months.

Criminal History
Minimum Sentence

Overall, the median minimum sentence for offenders under custody was more than 5 years.

However, the average minimum sentence length was ten years, reflecting the influence of lengthy minimum terms of many inmates. About one third are serving minimum sentences of 10 years or more.

Current sentencing laws in New York require an inmate convicted of certain crimes to receive a determinate sentence. Determinate sentences require an offender to serve a minimum term of 6/7 of the determinate sentence imposed by the judge before being eligible for release. An inmate committed for a crime not designated as having a determinate sentence has a minimum sentence set by the court.

As of January 1, 2014, there were 256 inmates under custody who were serving sentences of "Life without Parole." In calculating the average minimum sentence length, "Life without Parole" cases were given a value of 45 years or 540 months.

Minimum Sentence Length of Offenders
Length of Time to Earliest Release Date (Inmate Only 2014)

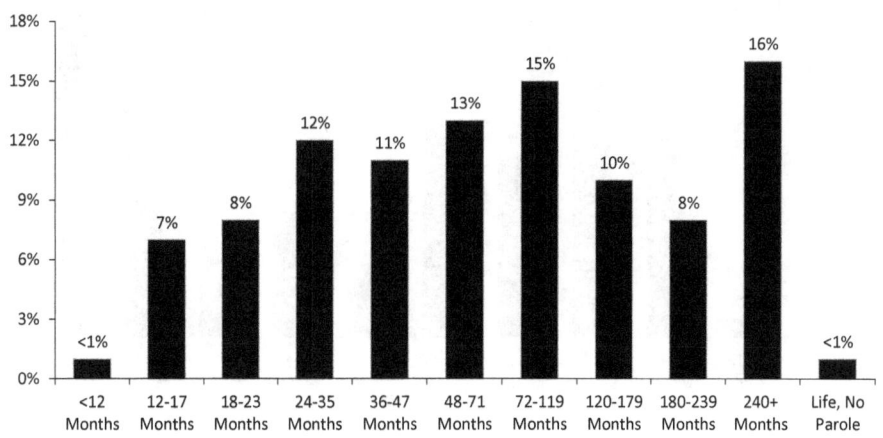

Maximum Sentence

As of January 1, 2014, the median maximum sentence of offenders under custody was 7 years (84 months). However, the average maximum sentence length was over eleven and a half years, reflecting the influence of lengthy maximum terms of many inmates. Almost a third had maximum sentences of 15 years or more with over 18% of the population having a maximum sentence of life.

Average maximum sentences for women (99 months) were 42 months shorter than for men (141 months). Median maximum sentences for women (60 months) were 24 months shorter than for men (84 months). Average maximum sentences for inmates (141 months) were 93 months shorter than for incarcerated parolees (48 months).

In calculating the average maximum sentence length, "Life without Parole" cases were given a value of 45 years or 540 months, and Life maximum cases were given a value of 25 years or 300 months.

Maximum Sentence Length of Offenders

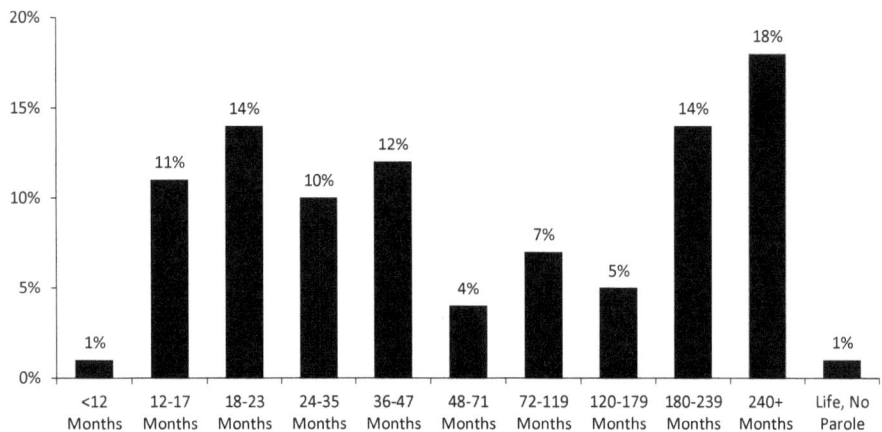

The median is the middle point between the number of instances of greater value and the number of instances of lesser value. The median is therefore less subject to the influence of extreme values than is the average and is preferred by some users for this reason

Chapter 17

American Civil Liberties Union

"Warehoused and Forgotten"
June 9, 2014

Warehoused and Forgotten: Immigrants Trapped in Our Shadow Private Prison System documents our multi-year investigation into five Criminal Alien Requirement (CAR) prisons run under contract with the federal Bureau of Prisons (BOP) in Texas. Our investigation uncovered evidence that the immigrants held in these private prisons are subjected to shocking abuse and mistreatment and discriminated against by BOP policies that impede family contact and exclude them from rehabilitative programs. Meanwhile, these private prisons operate in the shadows, effectively free from public scrutiny.

What are CAR prisons? Who is in them?

Criminal Alien Requirement (CAR) prisons are private prisons operated under contract with BOP to hold low-security, non-U.S.-citizen prisoners. Unlike most federal prisons—which are run as publicly accountable federal institutions by BOP—these prisons are operated by for-profit companies (Corrections Corporation of America, GEO Group, and Management & Training Corp.). There are thirteen CAR prisons around the country, located in Georgia, Mississippi, New Mexico, North Carolina, Ohio, Pennsylvania, and Texas.

Rising criminal prosecutions of immigrants for crossing the border, offenses previously handled almost entirely by the civil immigration system, are dramatically changing who enters the federal prison system—and fueling the growth of CAR prisons. Starting in 2009, more people entered federal prison for immigration offenses each year than for violent, weapons, and property offenses combined. By 2012, BOP was holding 23,700 people convicted of immigration offenses in its custody on a daily basis. People convicted of immigration offenses now represent one of the largest categories of people in CAR prisons and of non-citizens in BOP custody generally.

Our Privatization Problem

Mass incarceration has fueled the growth of the modern private prison industry—a multi-billion-dollar enterprise that depends on and profits from our national addiction to incarceration. From 1990 to 2009, as mass incarceration accelerated, the private prison industry grew by more than 1600%.

This growth has fueled rising fortunes in the private prison industry. The three corporations that operate CAR prisons nationwide—Corrections Corporation of America, the GEO Group (GEO), and MTC—reported nearly $4 billion in revenue in 2012. The private industry maximizes its profits by cutting costs where it can.

Cutting Corners to Increase Profits

Medical understaffing and extreme cost-cutting measures reportedly limit prisoners' access to both emergency and routine medical care. Martin, a 36-year old Cuban immigrant, told us he woke up in the middle of a severe asthma attack one night and did not have access to his inhaler. There was no doctor on staff that night, so he waited nearly an hour to see a nurse who did not know how to properly intubate him.

Hidden Component of Immigration System

The truth about what happens behind the walls of these private prisons often stays hidden. BOP subjects CAR prisons to insufficient oversight and accountability and exempts CAR prisons from many of the policies, rules, and regulations intended to set baselines of safe and humane treatment in federal prisons. Meanwhile, external oversight and accountability is frustrated by the isolation of prisoners from attorneys and legal services. BOP even assists private prison companies in efforts to block BOP's own records from public disclosure.

Cut off From Civilization

There is an overwhelming sense of despair at the CAR prisons we visited. Many of the men feel forgotten. They are far from family. They have little access to legal services. They feel like commodities exploited by the private prison companies that confine them. "You lose your memory in this place," one prisoner told us. "You keep counting days until you give up hope."

Chapter 18

"Is the United States a Racial Democracy?"

Jason Stanley and Vesla Weaver

"Starting in the 1970s, the United States has witnessed a drastic increase in the rate of black imprisonment, both absolutely and relative to whites." Therefore, in the decade after "the civil rights movement in the 1960s," in which blacks gained some equal formal rights under the law Stateside, the law increasingly needed to removed blacks from the streets and (because of voting rules governing felons and ex-felons) the body politic. Stanley and Weaver name this "a racial democracy," that is, a state that "unfairly applies the laws governing the removal of liberty primarily to citizens of one race, thereby singling out its members as especially unworthy of liberty, which they believed Blacks didn't have human dignity."

Even if the laws were not officially designed or enacted with this purpose, the pattern of consequences has long been visible in the statistics. Given human nature, it is likely that some (the insiders such as law-enforcement, corrections' staff / contractors, certain politicians, media, etc.) that benefit from this consequence probably noticed it before the people who do not obviously benefit from the new regime.

Human nature being what it is, often the disadvantaged outsiders are the first to speak up about the unintended side-consequence. The outsiders are at a disadvantage when they do so because if the side-consequence is really harmful they fight it with relatively trim resources while trying to figure out what the hell is going on. Meanwhile, the insiders can believe they have clean hands. While they actively benefit from an outcome pattern, they can always claim that none of them intended it or actively promoted this. Moreover, if the outcome pattern is endorsed by justice, why would one even imagine that something is incorrect?

Stanley and Weaver deploy the idea (attributed to Elizabeth Anderson) that sometimes our ideals prevent us from seeing the gap between our ideals and reality. This is really common sense: our most important commitments can cloud how we experience the world: our beloved is beautiful, our religion noble, our sports team best, etc. When our ideals also serve our interests this treacherous gap is even more likely.

Every political community needs some such mix of ideals and interest; these commitments provide the ongoing background stability of the right sort so that we can count on shared expectations. Some such expectations are, as Adam Smith argued, part of the psychological mechanism which facilitate our commitments to justice that govern the countless interactions and transactions that fall below the radar screen of the law and the variety of government surveillance. So, one can't easily promote a change in the application of the ideals without either confronting opposing interests or the stability of the community (or both). Once stability is threatened many of the well-meaning prefer the status quo, which is one reason why fear-mongering can be an effective tactic for organizations that are worried about their survival, or even relatively modest change.

In their piece, Stanley and Weaver are careful not to attack the principles, which they praise, themselves. While they are explicit about the political effects of racial democracy, they are careful not to blame the variety of agents and mechanisms that bring these effects about. For in a democracy the blame can be traced to one's fellow citizens (i.e., the active insiders and the majority of voters that support them). If one wants to reform one cannot insult one's potential allies and supporters.

So, in a democracy it is not just our ideals that makes us miss-perceive reality; we also have strategic reasons to keep quiet. But without some such publicity or gentle reminder from those that have worked through the social chain of causes, many of us will never see or grapple with the problem in full even if somewhere in the intellectual division of labor the information is fully available. So, the gap between ideal and reality may be kept somewhat wide for political reasons even by would be reformers. While truth-speaking is a norm of democracy, there are ways in which democracy may incline us not to say the whole truth.

Instead, Stanley and Weaver name the problem, describe the effects, and appeal to their readers' sense of fairness (a key word in their piece). The advantage of fairness is that it motivates in name of the very same ideals that are part of the problem. Machiavelli taught would be rulers to govern the passions by other passions. One can say that would be reformers attempt to improve the ideals by nearly identical ethics. As the history of successful reform suggests, this strategy can work very well. But in looking back at the transition between the civil rights movement in the 1960s and the increasing incarceration of blacks from the 1970s onward, one can also learn that if one fails to destroy the political powers that can cause oppression, one might just substitute one form of injustice with another.

"Is the United States a "Racial Democracy?

Dr. Stanley and his co-author, Dr. Vesla Weaver, argue that the disproportionate surveillance, imprisonment, and post-conviction voter disenfranchisement of black Americans threatens the very integrity of our democracy. On any given day, 5.85 million people are unable to vote because they are in prison, on parole, or disenfranchised as felons. A disproportionate percentage of them are black. Of the nation's 2.3 million prisoners, about 1 million are black, despite the fact that black people represent just 13% of the population. If current trends continue, 1 in 3 black men born today can expect to go to prison in his lifetime.

The essay raises pointed questions of interest to any skeptical citizen: Why do we strip prisoners of the right to vote in the first place? Does our fervent belief in democracy and equality blind us to the realities of our political system? Host Lindsay Beyerstein explores this question in this week's episode.

The New York Times article is co-authored with Yale University's leading expert on the prison system, who has a forthcoming book with Princeton University's second leading expert on the prison system. As is well-documented in the social psychology literature, racists suffer from the "naive realism effect", whereby immediately they think that anyone who does not share their racist views is ideological and not objective.

This is well-documented in social psychology, not just with racism, but with a range of 'hot button' political issues. As to facts, except for crack cocaine, black drug use by all measures is significantly lower than white drug use.

The addictive element in crack cocaine is cocaine, and powdered cocaine is a drug of choice among many white elite. Black murder rates are much higher than white murder rates. But that doesn't explain why blacks are incarcerated for non-violent drug offenses at ten times the rate at which whites are incarcerated for non-violent drug offenses. The sentencing disparities between blacks and whites for all crimes, violent and non-violent, are shockingly high. The commentators on this thread are white supremacists.

Chapter 19

Corporations, Crime and Justice, Economy

"This Is How Private Prison Companies Make Millions Even When Crime is Down"

Andy Kroll, September 19, 2013.

We are living in boom times for the private prison industry. The Corrections Corporation of America (CCA), the nation's largest owner of private prisons, has seen its revenue climb by more than 500 percent in the last two decades. And CCA wants to get much, much bigger: Last year, the company **made an offer** to 48 governors to buy and operate their state-funded prisons. But what made CCA's pitch to those governors so audacious and shocking was that it included a so-called occupancy requirement, a clause demanding the state keep those newly privatized prisons at least 90 percent full at all times, regardless of whether crime was rising or falling.

Occupancy requirements, as it turns out, are common practice within the private prison industry. A new report by In the Public Interest, an **anti-privatization group**, reviewed 62 contracts for private prisons operating around the country at the loc*POLITICAL MOJO*"al and state level. In the Public Interest found that 41 of those contracts included occupancy requirements mandating that local or state government keep those facilities between 80 and 100 percent full. In other words, whether crime is rising or falling, the state must keep those beds full. (The report was funded by **grants** from the **Open Society Institute** and **Public Welfare**, according to a spokesman.)

All the big private prison companies—CCA, GEO Group, and the Management and Training Corporation—try to include occupancy requirements in their contracts, according to the report.

States with the highest occupancy requirements include Arizona (three prison contracts with 100 percent occupancy guarantees), Oklahoma (three contracts with 98 percent occupancy guarantees), and Virginia (one contract with a 95 percent occupancy guarantee). At the same time, private prison companies **have supported and helped write** "three-strike" and "truth-in-sentencing" laws that drive up prison populations. Their livelihoods depend on towns, cities, and states sending more people to prison and keeping them there.

You might be wondering: What happens when crime drops and prison populations dwindle in states that agreed to keep their private prisons 80 percent or 90 percent full? Consider Colorado. The state's crime rate has sunk by a third in the past decade, and since 2009, five state-run prisons have shuttered because they weren't needed. Many more prison beds remain empty in other state facilities. Yet the state **chose not to fill those beds** because Democratic Gov. John Hickenlooper and CCA cut a deal to instead send 3,330 prisoners to CCA's three Colorado prisons. Colorado taxpayers foot the bill for leaving those state-run prisons underused. In March, Christie Donner, executive director of the Colorado **Criminal Justice** Reform Coalition, estimated that the state wasted at least $2 million in taxpayer money using CCA's prisons instead of its own.

That's just one example of how private prison companies keep the dollars rolling in, whether crime is rising or waning. Not surprisingly, In the Public Interest's report calls on local and state governments to refuse to include occupancy requirements and even ban such requirements with new legislation. "With governmental priorities pulling public funds in so many different **directions**, it makes no financial sense for taxpayers to fund empty prison beds," the report says.

Chapter 20

"Riker's Island New York City – Is one of the Worst Prison in America"

While people of color make up about 30 percent of the United States' population, they account for 60 percent of those imprisoned. The prison population grew by 700 percent from 1970 to 2005, a rate that is outpacing crime and population rates. The incarceration rates disproportionately impact men of color: 1 in every 15 African American men and 1 in every 36 Hispanic men are incarcerated in comparison to 1 in every 106 white men.

I can only image states like California, Texas, New York, Florida and Illinois would be targeting states which has the largest population of people living in them. New York City has a population of 8.4 million people living in it. Particularly in the poorer parts of the city where more non-white people reside.

The New York Metro Black population is the largest of any city in the United States at close to 3.5 million. This is almost 9% of the entire Black population of the United States. New York City has more than 2.4 million African Americans.

Evidence shows that minorities experience contact with the police at rates that far exceed their share of crime. One study found that the possibility that a black male 19 or 20 years of age will be stopped by police in New York City at least once during 2006 is 92 percent.

The probability for a Latino male of the same age group is 50 percent. For a young white man, it is 20 percent. In 90 percent of the stops of young minorities in 2011, there wasn't evidence of wrongdoing, and no arrest or citation occurred. In over half of the stops of minorities, the reason given for the stop was that the person made "furtive movements." In 60 percent of the stops, an additional reason listed for the stop was that the person was in a "high crime area."

Blacks are not essentially having these encounters at greater rates than their white counterparts because they are more criminal. Nationwide surveys show that, with the exclusion of crack cocaine, blacks consistently report using drugs at lower levels than whites. Some studies also suggest that blacks are engaged in drug transferring at lower levels. However once we account for their share of the population, blacks are 10 times as likely to spend time in prison for offenses related to drugs.

The "Three-Strike" and "Truth-in-Sentencing" laws could have a field's day with these states. Which I believe these laws were written for the purpose of locking people up longer than necessary to gain free labor. This is definitely another form of slavery and everyone should be outraged about our prison system in America. These practices are not only unfair to the prisoners, they are also unfair to the taxpayers. Meanwhile, large corporations are getting richer and richer while we are suffering and becoming poorer and poorer and more disfranchised.

If you understand that this country's foundation was built upon slavery, then you can understand it is impossible to get rid of this system without getting rid of the foundation. I put this book together, because I believe a lot of people are not aware of how our prison complex works.

Yes, I understand we have a lot of criminals out there, but why are we keeping non-violent offenders locked-up longer than necessary? One of the reason is because of its labor practices.

Paying them little to nothing per hour. Doesn't this cheat the working class people and taxpayers? This is not better than outsourcing work, this takes away jobs from the American's citizens, just think about it.

When serving time in prison it is not supposed to be enjoyable. Neither however, is it supposed to include being raped by other prisoners or staff members, being beaten by guards for the slightest provocation, driven mad by long-term solitary confinement, or killed off by medical carelessness. These are the fates of thousands of prisoners every year—men, women, and children housed in lockups that gives Gitmo and Abu Ghraib prisons a run for their money.

Riker's Island (New York City)

When it comes to shame, New York City's island lockup complex has it all: staff brutality, inmate violence, abuse of adolescents, rape, and the mentally ill, and one of the country's highest rates of solitary confinement. Riker's, which hosts 10 separate jails, has been the target of dozens of lawsuits and numerous exposés. So far the East River Island remains a despondent and dangerous residence for the 10,000 – 12,000 or more men, women, and children held there on any given day—mostly pretrial defendants who can't make bail and non-violent offenders with sentences too short to be sent upstate.

A 2012 lawsuit by the Legal Aid Society also documents a "deeply ingrained" pattern of violence by the guards, who "use unlawful, excessive force with impunity" and often send prisoners to the hospital, costing the city millions in legal settlements. Notwithstanding the alleged collaboration of staff in the rampant violence, the Department of Corrections' response has been to build more solitary cells at Riker's—nearly 1,000 in all, with special isolation units for adolescents and for people with mental illness.

Chapter 22

"6 Shocking Revelations about How Private Prisons Make Their Money"

April M. Short, September 20, 2013

Private prison companies are striking deals with states that contain clauses to guarantee high prison occupancy rates.

Imagine living in a country where prisons are private corporations that profit from keeping their beds stocked at, or near, capacity and the governing officials scramble to meet contractual "lockup quotas." Imagine that taxpayers would have to PAY for any empty beds should crime rates fall below that quota. Surprise! You already live there.

A new report from In the Public Interest (ITPI) revealed last week that private prison companies are striking deals with states that contain clauses guaranteeing high prison occupancy rates. The report, "Criminal: How Lockup Quotas and 'Low-Crime Taxes' Guarantee Profits for Private Prison Corporations," documents the contracts exchanged between private prison companies and state and local governments that either guarantee prison occupancy rates (essentially creating inmate lockup quotas) or force taxpayers to PAY for empty beds if the prison population decreases due to lower crime rates or other factors (essentially creating low-crime taxes).

Some of these contracts require 90 to 100 percent prison occupancy.

In a letter to 48 state governors in 2012, the largest for-profit private prison company in the US, Corrections Corporation of America (CCA), offered to buy up and operate public state prisons. In exchange, states would have to sign a 20-year contract guaranteeing a 90 percent occupancy rate throughout the term.

While no state accepted CCA's offer, a number of private prison companies have been inserting similar occupancy guarantee provisions into prison privatization contracts and requiring states to maintain high occupancy rates within their privately owned prisons. Three privately run prisons in Arizona have contracts that require 100 percent inmate occupancy, so the state is obligated to keep its prisons filled to capacity. Otherwise it has to pay the private company for any unused beds.

The report notes that contract clauses like this incentivize criminalization, and do nothing to promote rehabilitation, crime reduction or community building.

"[These contracts run] counter to many states' public policy goals of reducing the prison population and increasing efforts for inmate rehabilitation, "the report states." When policymakers received the 2012 CCA letter, some worried the terms of CCA's offer would encourage criminal justice officials to seek harsher sentences to maintain the occupancy rates required by a contract. Policy decisions should be based on creating and maintaining a just criminal justice system that protects the public interest, not ensuring corporate profits."

In a press teleconference about the report, Reverend Michael McBride, director of Urban Strategies and Lifelines to Healing at PICO National Network said the real human impact of having lockup quotas was unjustifiable.

"It's important for us to step back and look at this from a moral perspective; all people of any faith or no faith at all can claim it's reprehensible to imprison someone for MAKING MONEY or financial motives," he said. "It's important to always remember every single person is a human being ... even if they have done something we may find problematic or illegal. They are not profit incentives."

Here are six of the most shocking facts about prison privatization and corporatization, from the report.

1. 65 percent of the private prison contracts ITPI received and analyzed included occupancy guarantees in the form of quotas or required PAYMENTS for empty prison cells (a "low-crime tax"). These quotas and low-crime taxes put taxpayers on the hook for guaranteeing profits for private prison corporations.

2. Occupancy guarantee clauses in private prison contracts range between 80% and 100%, with 90% as the most frequent occupancy guarantee requirement.

3. Arizona, Louisiana, Oklahoma and Virginia are locked in contracts with the highest occupancy guarantee requirements, with all quotas requiring between 95% and 100% occupancy.

4. Though crime has dropped by a third in the past decade, an occupancy requirement covering three for-profit prisons has forced taxpayers in Colorado to pay an additional $2 million.

5. Three Arizona for-profit prison contracts have a staggering 100% quota, even though a 2012 analysis from Tucson Citizen shows that the company's per-day charge for each prisoner has increased an average of 13.9% over the life of the contracts.

6. A 20-year deal to privately operate the Lake Erie Correctional Institution in Ohio includes a 90% quota, and has contributed to cutting corners on safety, including overcrowding, areas without SECURE doors and an increase in crime both inside the prison and in the surrounding community.

Chapter 23

How Many Individuals with Serious Mental Illness are in Jails and Prisons?
(Updated November 2014)

SUMMARY:

Approximately 20 percent of inmates in jails and 15 percent of inmates in state prisons have a serious mental illness. Based on the total number of inmates, this means that there are approximately 356,000 inmates with serious mental illness in jails and state prisons. This is 10 times more than the approximately 35,000 individuals with serious mental illness remaining in state hospitals.[1]

How many individuals with serious mental illness are in jails?

A study published in 2009, based on inmate interviews in jails in Maryland and New York, reported that 16.7 percent of the inmates (14.5 percent of males and 31 percent of females) had symptoms of a serious mental illness (schizophrenia, schizo-affective, bipolar disorder, major depression, brief psychotic disorder) within the previous month. However, another 31 percent of the inmates who were asked to participate in the study refused; this group almost certainly included many individuals with paranoid schizophrenia. Since the situation has gotten worse since the interviews in this study were done between 2002 and 2006, and given the high rate of refusers, it seems reasonable to estimate that at this time approximately 20 percent of jail inmates have a serious mental illness.[2]

How many individuals with serious mental illness are in state prisons?

A 2006 survey carried out by the U.S. Department of Justice reported that "an estimated 10 percent of State prisoners...reported symptoms that met criteria for a psychotic disorder." This survey was based on 2004 data and the situation has gotten worse since then. Thus, 15 percent would appear a conservative estimate.[3]

In 2012 there were 744,524 inmates in county and city jails. If 20 percent of them had a serious mental illness, that would make a total of approximately 149,000 jail inmates with a serious mental illness.

In 2011 there were 1,382,418 inmates in state prisons. If 15 percent of them had a serious mental illness, that would make a total of approximately 207,000 state prison inmates with a serious mental illness.

If the number of jail and state prison inmates with a serious mental illness were added together, they total approximately 356,000 inmates. Since there are only approximately 35,000 individuals with serious mental illness remaining in state mental hospitals, there are now 10 times more individuals with serious mental illness in jails and state prisons than there are in state mental hospitals.

The nation's jails and prisons have replaced hospitals as the primary facility for mentally ill individuals.[4]

There are more seriously mentally ill individuals in the Los Angeles County Jail, Chicago's Cook County Jail, or New York's Riker's Island Jail than in any psychiatric hospital in the United States. In fact, in every county in the US that has both a county jail and a county psychiatric facility, the jail has more seriously mentally ill individuals. A 2004–2005 survey reported that there were "more than three times more seriously mentally ill persons in jails and prisons than in hospitals."[5]

The average stay for mentally ill inmates in jail is longer than for non–mentally ill inmates. In Florida's Orange County Jail, the average stay for all inmates is 26 days; for mentally ill inmates, it is 51 days. In New York's Riker's Island Jail, the average stay for all inmates is 42 days; for mentally ill inmates, it is 215 days. The main reason mentally ill inmates stay longer is that many find it difficult to understand and follow jail and prison rules. In one study, jail inmates were twice as likely (19 percent versus 9 percent) to be charged with facility rule violations. In another study in the Washington State prisons, mentally ill inmates accounted for 41 percent of infractions even though they constituted only 19 percent of the prison population. Another reason mentally ill inmates stay longer is that they are often held for months awaiting the availability of a bed in a psychiatric hospital.[6]

Mentally ill inmates cost more. Mentally ill inmates cost more than non–mentally ill inmates for a variety of reasons, including increased staffing needs. In Broward County, Florida, it costs $80 a day to house a regular inmate but $130 a day for an inmate with mental illness. In Texas prisons "the average prisoner costs the state about $22,000 a year," but "prisoners with mental illness range from $30,000 to $50,000 a year." Psychiatric medications are a significant part of the increased costs; in July of 2002 at Ohio's Clark County Jail, prescription drugs costs for inmates exceeded the costs of feeding inmates. Finally, there is the cost of an increasing number of lawsuits, such as the suit brought in New Jersey in 2006 by the family of a "65-year-old mentally ill stockbroker [who was] stomped to death in the Camden County Jail."[7]

Mentally ill inmates are often major management problems. Because of their impaired thinking, many inmates with serious mental illnesses are major management problems. For example, in 2005 in Mississippi's Hinds County Jail, one inmate was described as having "tore up a damn padded cell that's indestructible, and he ate the cover of the damn padded cell. We took his clothes and gave him a paper suit to wear, and he ate that. When they fed him food in a styrofoam container, he ate that. We had his stomach pumped six times, and he's been operated on twice." In Wisconsin a 2010 audit of three state prisons reported that "between 55 percent and 76 percent of inmates in segregation [isolation] are mentally ill."[8]

Mentally ill inmates are more likely to commit suicide. Multiple studies have shown that approximately half of all inmate suicides are committed by inmates who are seriously mentally ill. A 2002 study in Washington State reported that "the prevalence of mental illness among inmates who attempted suicide was 77 percent, compared with 15 percent [among inmates] in the general jail population." In California in 2002, the Los Angeles Times headlined: "Jail Suicides Reach Record Pace in State," and added: "Some experts blame the recent surge on forcing more of the mentally ill behind bars."[9]

ICPS International Centre for Prison Studies
Highest to Lowest - Prison Population Total (30 Countries)

Ranking	Title	Prison Population Total
1.	United States of America	2,217,000
2.	China	1,657,812
3.	Russian Federation	673,818
4.	Brazil	581,507
5.	India	411,991
6.	Thailand	330,923
7.	Mexico	255,638
8.	Iran	225,624
9.	Indonesia	167,163
10.	Turkey	165,033
11.	South Africa	157,824
12.	Vietnam	142,636
13.	Colombia	116.760
14.	Philippines	110,925
15.	Ethiopia	93,044
16.	UK: England & Wales	85,681
17.	Poland	78.013
18.	Pakistan	74,944
19.	Morocco	72,816
20.	Ukraine	72,278
21.	Peru	71,961
22.	Bangladesh	71,606
23.	France	66,270
24.	Spain	65,375
25.	Argentina	64,288
26.	Taiwan	64,104
27.	Egypt	62,000
28.	Germany	61,872
29.	Japan	61,794
30.	Algeria	60,220

http://www.prisonstudies.org/highest-to-lowest/prison-population
total?field_region_taxonomy_tid=All

Conclusion

I hope after reading this book, we all have a better understanding of our Justice system. As well as the prison complex. How they treat us as African/Black Americans. They never planned justice for us as a people. So let's stop judging our African/Black men/women with sure a critical mind/eye and with more understanding then we had before reading this book.

Mass Incarceration

Race, Prison, and Poverty, Paul Street

According to "get-tough on crime" politicians and policy-makers, "prison works": it reduces crime rates. But that intuitively seductive argument, which cites the declining federal crime index of the 1990s as its primary evidence, cannot explain why crime rates increased in the 1970s and the late 1980s while prison rates grew at the same rate as they did in the 1990s. It ignores the fact that drug convictions do not figure into the federal index a crucial omission since incarceration rates are strongly fed by the "war on drugs." It ignores the strong possibility that other factors, including the record-length economic expansion of the 1990s, provide better explanations than mass incarceration for declining official crime. It is embarrassed, finally, by comparative international data. U.S. citizens are just as likely to be victimized by crime as citizens in European countries who jail and imprison relatively tiny percentages of their population because they view prisons as fundamentally criminogenic as breeders of crime. Americans are far more likely than their low-incarceration European counterparts to be victimized by rape, murder, robbery, and violent assault in general.

Part of the Tangle

It is no simple matter to determine the precise extent to which mass incarceration is exacerbating the deep socio-economic and related cultural and political traumas that already plague inner-city communities and help explain disproportionate Black "criminality," arrest, and incarceration in the first place. Still, it is undeniable that the race to incarcerate is having a profoundly negative effect on Black communities. Equally undeniable is the fact that Black incarceration rates reflect deep racial bias in the criminal justice system and the broader society. Do the cheerleaders of "get tough" crime and sentencing policy really believe that African-Americans deserve to suffer so disproportionately at the hands of the criminal justice system? There is a vast literature showing that structural, institutional, and cultural racism and severe segregation by race and CLASS ARE leading causes of inner-city crime. Another considerable body of literature shows that Blacks are victims of racial bias at every level of the criminal justice system from stop, frisk, and arrest to prosecution, sentencing, release, and execution. These disparities give legitimacy to the movement of ex-offender groups for the expungement of criminal and prison records for many nonviolent offenses, especially in cases where ex-convicts have shown an earnest desire to "go straight." Further and deeper remedies will be required. These include a moratorium on new prison construction (to stop the insidious, self-replicating expansion of the prison-industrial complex), the repeal of laws that deny voting rights to felons and ex-felons, amnesty and release for most inmates convicted of non-violent crimes, de-criminalization of narcotics, the repeal of the "war on drugs" at home and abroad, revision of state and federal sentencing and local "zero tolerance" practices and ordinances, abolition of racial, ethnic, and class profiling in police practice, and the outlawing of private, for-profit prisons and other economic activities that derive investment gain from mass incarceration.

Activists and policy makers should call and make plans for a criminal- to social-justice "peace dividend" the large-scale transfer of funds spent on mass arrest, surveillance, and incarceration into such policy areas as drug treatment, job-training, transitional services for ex-offenders, and public education regarding the employment potential of ex-offenders. They should call and make plans for the diversion of criminal justice resources from "crime in the streets" (i.e., the harassment and imprisonment of lower- class and inner-city people) to serious engagement with under-sentenced "crime in the suites." More broadly, they should seek a general redistribution of resources from privileged and often fantastically wealthy persons to those most penalized from birth by America's long and intertwined history of inherited class and race privilege.

America's expanding prison, probation, and parole populations are recruited especially from what leading slavery reparations advocate Randall Robinson calls "the millions of African-Americans bottom-mired in urban hells by the savage time-release social debilitations of American slavery." The ultimate solutions lay, perhaps, beyond the parameters of the existing politic-economic order. "Capitalism," Eugene Debs argued in 1920, "needs and must have the prison to protect itself from the [lower-class] criminals it has created." But the examples of Western Europe and CANADA, where policy makers prefer prevention and rehabilitation through more social-democratic approaches, show that mass incarceration is hardly an inevitable product of capitalism per se. Nothing can excuse policymakers and activists from the responsibility to end racist criminal justice practices that are significantly exacerbating the difficulties faced by the nation's most truly and intractably disadvantaged. More than merely a symptom of the tangled mess of problems that create, sustain, and deepen America's savage patterns of class and race inequality, mass incarceration has become a central part of the mess. For these and other reasons, it will be an especially worthy target for creative, democratic protest and policy formation in the new millennium.

REFERENCECS:

Introduction – *Department of Corrections and Community Supervision.* Retrieved from http://www.doccs.ny.gov/[1]

Saturday, 28 March 2015. Federal Bureau of Prisons. Retrieved from http://www.bop.gov/about/statistics/statistics_inmate_race.jsp[2]

PBS.org. SLAVERY by another Name. Retrieved from http://www.pbs.org/tpt/slavery-by-another-name/themes/chain-gangs/[3]

"Used by permission, Twin Cities Public Television © 2012"

Chris Hedges, A. Dec 28, 2014. *The Prison State of America.* Retrieved from http://www.truthdig.com/report/item/the_prison_state_of_america_2014122 8 [4]

Chapter 1 – Jaron Browne, A., *Rooted in Slavery: Prison Labor Exploitation.* Retrieved from http://reimagineorg/node/856

Chapter 2 – Black Men Are Missing: *Tell Us Something We Don't Know* – Peniele E. Joseph Retrieved from http://www.theroot.com/articles/politics/2015/04/black_men_are_missing_t ell_us_something _we_don_t_know.html

Chapter 3 – *Prisoners for Profit: "CUNY Prison Divest and the Carceral State".* Retrieved from http://opencuny.org/theadvocate/2015/04/29/prisoners-for-profit-cuny-prison-divest-and-the carceral-state/

Chapter 4 – *Department of Corrections and Community Supervision.*[1] Retrieved from http://www.doccs.ny.gov/Research/Reports/2014/UnderCustody_Report_2 014.pdf – *Equal Justice Initiative.* Retrieved from http://racialinjustice.eji.org/timeline/1860s/[2]

Chapter 5 – Government uses Prison Labor to make Military Uniforms

Chapter 6 – NAACP – *Incarceration Trends in America.* Retrieved from http://www.naacp.org/pages/criminal-justice-fact-sheet

Chapter 7 – **Lucas Reilly** – TheRichest – *10 Products You Didn't Know Were Made By Prisoners. Retrieved from* http://www.therichest.com/rich-list/most-shocking/10-products-you-didnt-know-were-made-by-prisoners/ Retrieved by http://www.therichest.com/rich-list/most-shocking/5-clothing-brands-that-are-manufactured-in-prison/?view=all

Chapter 8 – *"21st-Century Slaves: How Corporations Exploit Prison Labor" AlterNet* – Retrieved from http://www.alternet.org/story/151732/21st-century_slaves%3A_how_corporations_exploit_prison_labor

Chapter 9 – *"Companies That Get Rich off Prisoners"* – *http://www.privateci.org/rap_aramark.html*

Chapter 10 – *"The Cost(s) of Incarceration"* By Steve Rempe, October 24, 2013 Retrieved from http://www.prisonfellowship.org/2013/10/the-costs-of-incarceration/

Chapter 11 – *New York State Special Commission.* Retrieved from http://www.correctionhistory.org/html/chronicl/state/html/nyprisons.html

Chapter 12 – Adrian Smith. Published June 11, 2012. *Private vs. Public Facilities, Is it cost effective and safe? Retrieved from* http://www.corrections.com/news/article/30903-private-vs-public-facilities-is-it-cost-effective-and-safe-

Chapter 13 – Michael Snyder, March 11, 2013. Private Prisons: *The More Americans They Put Behind Bars the More Money They Make* (1) Timesleader.com
Retrieved from (2) http://theeconomiccollapseblog.com/archives/private-prisons-the-more-americans-they-put-behind-bars-the-more-money-they-make

Chapter 14 – Marc Mauer, Executive Director, and Ryan S. King, Policy Analyst, respectively, of *The Sentencing Project.* Retrieved from http://www.sentencingproject.org/doc/publications/rd_stateratesofincbyrace andethnicity.pdf

Chapter 15 – Brian Magee is the communications associate for the American Humanist Association. Retrieved from http://americanhumanist.org/hnn/details/2012-08-the-greed-of-private-prisons

Chapter 16 – *State of New York Department of Corrections and Community Supervision.* Retrieved from http://www.doccs.ny.gov/Research/Reports/2014/UnderCustody_Report_2 014.pdf

Chapter 17 – Warehoused and Forgotten "Immigrants Trapped in Our Shadow – Private Prison System" – American Civil Liberties Union – 212 549-2500 – Communications Dept. Eric Wojcki – Retrieved from http://www.aclutx.org/2014/06/09/warehoused-and-forgotten/

Chapter 18 – "Is the United States a Racializing Our Democracy?"– Retrieved from http://digressionsnimpressions.typepad.com/digressionsimpressions/2014/ 01/racialized-democracy-and-fairness.html

Chapter 19 – Andy Kroll, September 19, 2013. *This Is How Private Prison Companies Make Millions Even When Crime Rates Fall* Retrieved from http://www.motherjones.com/mojo/2013/09/private-prisons-occupancy-quota-cca-crime

Chapter 20 – One of the Worst Prisons in America – Riker's Island in New York City

Chapter 21 – April M. Short, September 20, 2013. *6 Shocking Revelations About How Private Prisons Make Their Money.* Retrieved from http://www.alternet.org/civil-liberties/6-shocking-revelations-about-how-private-prisons-make-their-money

Chapter 22 – Retrieved from http://www.treatmentadvocacycenter.org/problem/consequences-of-non-treatment/2580

Conclusion: – Paul Street is research director at the Chicago Urban League Retrieved from
http://www.historyisaweapon.com/defcon1/streeracpripov.html

REFERENCECS:

Introduction – *Department of Corrections and Community Supervision.* Retrieved from http://www.doccs.ny.gov/[1]

Saturday, 28 March 2015. Federal Bureau of Prisons. Retrieved from http://www.bop.gov/about/statistics/statistics_inmate_race.jsp[2]

PBS.org. SLAVERY by Another Name. Retrieved from http://www.pbs.org/tpt/slavery-by-another-name/themes/chain-gangs/[3]

"Used by permission, Twin Cities Public Television © 2012"

Chris Hedges, A. Dec 28, 2014. *The Prison State of America.* Retrieved from http://www.truthdig.com/report/item/the_prison_state_of_america_2014122 8 [4]

Endnotes:

Chapter 1

Jaron Browne. *"Rooted in Slavery: Prison Labor Exploitation"*

1. There are more than 46 Black men in prison nationwide per 1000 Black men in the population, whereas the rate for white men is four per 1000. Democracy Now, "United States prison population jumps 3.7 percent to two million; Increase of 700 INMATES every week," Wednesday, July 30, 2003.

2. Erlich, Reese, "Prison Labor: Workin' For The Man." Covert Action Quarterly #54, Fall 1995.

3. In Tennessee, for example, African Americans were only 33 percent of the prison population in 1865, by 1877 the NUMBER had swelled to 67 percent of the total prison population. Shelden, Randall G., "Slavery in the 3rd Millennium Part II—Prisons and Convict Leasing Help Perpetuate Slavery," The Black Commentator, Issue 142, June 16, 2005.

4. Green, Fletcher M., "Some Aspects of the Convict Lease System in the Southern States," ESSAYS in Southern HISTORY, vol. 31, (Durham: University of North Carolina Press), 1949, pp. 116-120.

5. Hartnett, Stephen, "Prison Labor, Slavery & Capitalism In Historical Perspective" (c. 1997) referencing, Novak, D.A., The Wheel of Servitude: Black Forced Labor After Slavery.

6. Lichtenstein, Alexander, "Good Roads and Chain Gangs in the Progressive South: The Negro Convict is a Slave," The Journal of Southern History, (Athens, Georgia: Southern Historical Association), 1993, p. 87.

7. Wilson, Walter, Forced Labor in the United States, (New York: AMS Press, Inc.), 1933, p. 68.

8. Prison Law Office, The California State Prisoners Handbook, Section 3.17, pp. 79-80.

9. Reuters. "Sheriff runs female chain gang." www.cnn.com, October 29, 2003.

10. POWER is a San Francisco-based multiracial organization of low-wage workers and tenants. FOR MORE INFORMATION, see www.unite-to-fight.org.

Endnotes

Chapter 11 – *New York State Special Commission*

1. The President's Commission on Law Enforcement and Administration of Justice, *Task Force Report; Corrections* (Washington, D.C. US Government Printing Office, 1967), p. 4, reported, "Sixty-nine prisons opened before 1900 are still in use."

2. David Rothman, *The Discovery of the Asylum* (Boston, Little, Brown, 1971), p. 62

3. G.A. de Beaumont and A. de Tocqueville, *On the Penitentiary System in the United States and its Application in France* (Carbondale, Ill. Southern Illinois University Press. 1964), p. 59

4. Elizabeth Benz Croft, *New York State Prisons and Prison Riots from Auburn and Clinton: 1929 to Attica: 1971,* unpublished paper prepared for the School of Criminal Justice, State University of New York at Albany, March 30, 1972, p.15

5. Quoted by Rothman, *The Discovery of the Asylum*, p. 88

6. Ibid.

7. De Beaumont and de Tocqueville, *On the Penitentiary*

8. H. E. Barnes and N. K. Teeters, *New Horizons in Criminology* (Englewood Cliffs, N.J.; Prentice-Hall, 1951), pp. 524?25.

9. G. David Garson, *The Disruption of Prison Administration: An Investigation on Alternative Theories of the Relationship Among Administrators, Reformers, and Involuntary Social Service Clients,* paper prepared for delivery at the 1971 annual meeting of the American Political Science Association. Copyright American Political Science Association 1971, pp. 7, 8.

10. New York Department of Correction, "These Are Your New York State Correctional Institutions: Attica State Prison," 1949, p.5.

11. Except as otherwise indicated, the description of the correction system in 1971 prevailed up to the time of this report.

12. This is no longer universally true; since the Attica uprising, limited evening recreation programs have been introduced.

13. There were also medium security accommodations for a limited number of inmates operated within the maximum security prisons at Attica and at Clinton, where there was a 125 bed diagnostic and treatment center.

14. All new inmates are delivered to the Department of Correctional Services at one of three receiving institutions serving different areas of the state: Attica, Ossining, and Clinton; while inmates are tested here for the purpose of determining the appropriate institution to serve their sentences, the choice is limited to what is available, or, in almost all cases, the maximum security institution regardless of the results of the inmate's evaluation.

15. *Preliminary Report of the New York State Governor's Special Committee on Criminal Offenders* (New York: June 1968), p. 216.

Endnotes

Chapter 14 – *The sentencing Project*

1. See, for example, Ryan S. King, Marc Mauer, and Malcolm C. Young, Incarceration and Crime: A Complex Relationship, The Sentencing Project, 2005.

2. Thomas P. Bonczar, Prevalence of Imprisonment in the U.S. Population, 1974-2001, Bureau of Justice Statistics, 2003, p. 8.

3. See, for example, The Sentencing Project, Women in the Criminal Justice System, May 2007.

4. Hispanic is considered an ethnic category that is exclusive with the racial categories of black and white. We use the term "Hispanic" rather than "Latino" to follow BJS terminology.

5. Louis W. Jankowski, Correctional Populations in the United States, 1990, Bureau of Justice Statistics, 1992, p. 86; Paige M. Harrison and Allen J. Beck, Prisoners in 2005, Bureau of Justice Statistics, 2006, p. 8.6

6. Bonczar, supra note 2.

7. See, among others: Alfred Blumstein, "Racial Disproportionality of U.S. Prison Populations Revisited," University of Colorado Law Review, Vol. 64, No. 3, 1993; Michael Tonry, "Racial Disproportions in US Prisons," British Journal of Criminology, Vol. 34, 1994; Marc Mauer, "Intended and Unintended Consequences: State Racial Disparities in Imprisonment," The Sentencing Project, January 1997; Jamie Fellner, "Punishment and Prejudice: The Racial Costs in the War on Drugs," Human Rights Watch, May 2000.

8. Data for Native Americans, Asian Americans, and other racial groups are not available for analysis.

9. Except as otherwise noted, all incarceration data presented in this report are from Paige M. Harrison and Allen J. Beck, *Prison and Jail Inmates at Midyear 2005*, Bureau of Justice Statistics, 2006, p. 11

10. William J. Sabol, Todd D. Minton, and Paige M. Harrison, Prison and Jail Inmates at Midyear 2006, Bureau of Justice Statistics, 2007, p. 9

11. Census block groups represent between 1,000 and 3,000 residents.

12. James P. Lynch and William J. Sabol, Prisoner Reentry in Perspective, The Urban Institute, 2001, p. 16.

Endnotes

Chapter 22 – "*How Many Individuals with Serious Mental Illness are in Jails and Prisons?*

1. Torrey EF, Zdanowicz MT, Kennard AD et al. The treatment of persons with mental illness in prisons and jails: A state survey. Arlington, VA, Treatment Advocacy Center, April 8, 2014

2. Steadman, HJ, Osher, FC, Robbins, PC et al., Prevelenace of serious mental illness among jail inmates. *Psychiatric Services.* 2009; 60: 761-765

3. James, DJ, Glaze, LE. Mental health problems of prison and jail inmates. Special Report, Bureau of Justice Statistics. September 2006. NCJ 213600.

4. Torrey, EF, Zdanowicz, MT, Kennard, AD et al. The treatment of persons with mental illness in prison and jails: a state survey. Treatment Advocacy Center and National Sheriffs Association, April 8, 2014.

5. Torrey EF, Kennard AD, Eslinger D et al. *More Mentally Ill Persons Are in Jails and Prisons than Hospitals*: A Survey of the States (Arlington, VA.: Treatment Advocacy Center, 2010).\

6. Jails and mental illness, Criminal Justice/Mental Health Consensus Project, **http://consensusprojectorg/infocenter/facts.fafct_jails**, last accessed April 3, 206.
   Turner C. Ethical issues in criminal justice administration, *American Jails*, January/February 2007.
   Butterfield F. Study finds hundreds of thousands of inmates mental ill, *New York Times*, October 22, 2003.

7. Miller CM, Fantz A. Special "psych" jails planned, Miami Herald, November 15, 2007.
   Bender E. Community treatment more humane, reduces criminal-justice costs. *Psychiatric News* 2003;38:28.|
   Gottschlich AJ, Cetnar G. Drug bills at jail top food costs, Springfield [OH] News Sun, August 20, 2002.
   Guenther A. Family sues Camco over prisoner's death, *[NJ] Courier Post*, June 14, 2006.

8. Mitchell J. Treatment, no jail, urged for mentally ill in Miss., *Jackson [MS] Clarion Ledger*, January 25, 2009.
    Ridgeway J, Casella J. Locking down the mental ill, The Real Cost of Prisons Weblog, February 24, 2010, *http//realcostofprisons.org/blog/archieves/2010/locking_down_th.html*, last accessed April 28, 2011.

9. Goss JR, Peterson K, Smith LW et al. Characteristics of suicide attempts in a large urban jail system with an established suicide prevention program, Psychiatric Services 2002;53:574-579.
    Johnson J. Jail suicides reach record pace in state, *Los Angeles Times*, June 16, 2002.

Sources:

Chapter 12 – "*Private vs. Public Facilities, Is it cost effective and safe?***"**

Charles Campbell, "The Intolerable Hulks." (2001)

E. Bates, "Private Prisons," The Nation, Jan. 5, 1998, p. 13.

Good Jobs First, JAIL BREAKS: Economic Development Subsidies Given to Private Prisons," October 2001, p. 2.

J. Austin and G. Coventry, "Emerging Issues on Privatized Prisons," Bureau of Justice Assistance, February 2001.

Schmalleger, F., & Smykla, J. (2007, 2005, 2002). Corrections in the 21st Century. New York: McGraw-Hill.

The Sentencing Project, "Prison Privatization and the Use of Incarceration" (2004)

Todd, W. (2005). Convict Lease System. In The New Georgia Encyclopedia. Retrieved March 26, 2011, from http://www.georgiaencyclopedia.org/nge/Article.jsp? Id=h-2635

Corrections.com author, Adrian Smith, is a Classification Officer for Orange County Corrections in Orlando, Fl. He holds a Bachelors of Science Degree in Criminal Justice from Upper Iowa University and a MASTERS OF Science Degree in Criminal Justice from Everest University. He is currently obtaining his Doctorial Degree in Public Safety Leadership from Capella University. Adrian has been in Corrections for 6 years working for Florida's Prison and Jail system. He can be reached at Adrian.Smith@ocfl.net

Acknowledgement

I wish to personally thank the following people for their contributions to my inspiration and knowledge and other help in creating this book:

Deborah McDonald-Jackson

Denise Powell

Thank you to the following individuals who without their contributions and support this book would not have been written:

Jaron Browne

Chris Hedges

Steve Rempe

James Ridgeway

Michael Snyder

Adrian Smith

Jason Stanley & Vesla Weaver

Paul Street – Director at the Chicago Urban League

We hereby acknowledge the following people and organizations for their contributions to this book:

AlterNet – Rania Khalek

American Civil Liberties Union

The American Humanist Association – Brian Magee

CUNY

Equal Justice Initiative

Mother Jones

The NAACP

Twin Cities Public Television © 2012

The Richest

The Root

Univison Communities Inc.